# Women Who Carried the Good News

*For Angus*

# Women Who Carried the Good News

Eleanor Hull

Judson Press, Valley Forge

WOMEN WHO CARRIED THE GOOD NEWS



Translations of the Bible quoted in this book are as follows:

*The Holy Bible,* King James Version.

*The Holy Bible,* the Revised Standard Version of the Bible, © 1946 and 1952 by the Division of Christian Education of the National Council of the Churches of Christ in the United States of America. Used by permission.

---

**Library of Congress Cataloging in Publication Data**

Hull, Eleanor Means.
   Women who carried the good news.

   Includes bibliographical references.
   1. American Baptist Home Mission Societies.
   2. Missionaries, Women. I. Title.
BV2766.B48    266'.6'131    74-22520
ISBN 0-8170-0651-6

---

Printed in the U.S.A.

# Preface

This is the story of women's efforts in the past century to interpret the love of Christ to all North America. It is particularly American Baptist women's story, as they began their mission work in four separate cooperating units, organized respectively by Michigan women, Free Baptist women, Chicago-area women, and New England women. Collectively they are referred to here as the Woman's American Baptist Home Mission Society. This name was adopted when the units merged in 1909 and was used until 1955 when the American Baptist Home Mission Society and the Woman's American Baptist Home Mission Society came together as the American Baptist Home Mission Society. The story parallels the great Protestant missionary movement of the nineteenth century and is inextricably intertwined with the tumultuous history of the times.

The story follows the upward surge of power and accomplishment by women in missions in the "Women's Century" and the decline of women's initiative when their own organizations were integrated with those controlled by men. And then it looks with hope to the beginning of a new resurgence of women as they again become active in mission.

There have been several great periods of mission, from the pure individualism of the apostolic and medieval eras to the ecclesiastical Roman Catholic crusades and early Protestant state missions. But the latest and, according to Robert H. Glover, the greatest era has been that of *associate organization* which began with William Carey at Kettering. The women's missionary movement has been peculiarly expressive of this method as independent individuals have associated themselves in organizations for mutual action.

Thus each nurse, teacher, Christian Center worker, or pastor, has been indispensable. And there have been thousands! Only a few names can be mentioned here, only a few stories told. May the echoes from each reader's experience resonate with the text, and may each mind create rich variations on what is written here.

# Contents

Psalm 68:11
"The Lord gave the word; great was the company of those that published it." (KJV)


"The Lord gives the command;
    great is the host of those who bore the tidings." (RSV)


*"El Senor daba palabra, de las evangelizantes habia gran ejercito."*
(Spanish Version)
Translation: "The Lord gave the word; of the women carrying the message, there was a great army."

# Part One
# A Fire Exists by Burning

---

*"The church exists by mission,*
*just as a fire exists by burning."**
Emil Brunner

*Emil Brunner, *The Word and the World* (London: SCM Press, 1931), p. 108, as quoted in Gerald H. Anderson, ed., *The Theology of the Christian Mission* (New York: McGraw-Hill Book Co., Inc., 1961), p. 79.

# 1
# God Almighty's New Year

Sometime in November, Joanna landed on Island No. 10. She had never spoken to a black person but once in her life.

"Miss Moore, since you came here to make people good, try your hand on these women," suggested Captain Thomas.

Two women were fighting. They were almost naked, like most of the other thousand wretched black women and children herded into cabins and tents on this island in the mouth of the Mississippi River. Every fire and cooking pot had to be shared among twenty or thirty people. It was the glorious year of 1863.

"God Almighty's New Year" was what they called it, the four million triumphant black slaves, at last vindicated as persons. They were not slaves any longer; they were freedmen.

On January 1, at Tremont Temple in Boston the Abolitionists had lifted their voices in jubilation.

> Sound the loud timbrel of Egypt's dark sea,
> Jehovah hath triumphed, his people are free! [1]

Lincoln had ordered the raising of Negro troops and later proclaimed that the two hundred thousand who responded to his call had turned the tide for the Union.

But all was not won. The South continued to fight. The army of former slaves that stumbled northward was a nondescript horde of women and children and old men: an Exodus, Levi Coffin called it, without a Moses. Ben Butler called them "contraband," and under this precarious classification they flocked through snipers' bullet fire into Cincinnati, Ohio, and Cairo, Illinois, with no resources and diminishing hope. The Quaker Western Freedmen's Aid Committee came into being, largely made up of the same people who had risked their lives for years running the Underground Railway. They helped form colonies of the bewildered and exhausted refugees, and they sent out calls for food, clothing, and helpers.

Joanna P. Moore, a girl studying at Rockford Seminary in Illinois, had heard from a visiting speaker about the refugees who had been transferred from Cairo to Island No. 10.

"What can a man do to help such a suffering mass of humanity?" the impassioned speaker had demanded. "Nothing. A woman is needed, and nothing else will do."[2]

Wild thoughts had run through Joanna's mind as she listened to the speaker. As a child in a large, poor family, she had always helped. After becoming a Baptist at twenty, she had wanted to be a missionary. What was this but a missionary call?

She asked herself, "What can I, a poor child, do? What kind of people are they? Why did God let them be slaves and shut the door of knowledge to them for so many years? Will they listen to me? I have nothing to give them; I suppose God will show me how to love them. Every heart needs love. Yes, I expect I can love them, but they need something more substantial than love. There are many older and wiser than I . . . *What shall I do?*"[3]

She got only one answer: "Go and see and God will go with you."[4] The Sunday school of the First Baptist Church of Belvidere, Illinois, to which she belonged, pledged her four dollars a month, and the government gave her transportation and soldier's rations. The American Baptist Home Mission Society gave her a commission, but no salary.

The American Baptists, along with other denominations, were beginning to wake from thirty years of coma and were beginning to feel compelled to promote the evangelization and education of the freedmen. Each day brought more exposure of their needs and a deeper realization of the crimes of slavery. In proportion to their small black constituency, the Congregationalists responded most substantially, but the Baptists felt great responsibility, as their informal and enthusiastic style of worship had attracted the largest black membership.

"No great moral challenge equal to it has ever come to the American Church, and no small part of the power and vigor which the church had from 1870 to 1915 came as a result of its response to this challenge,"[5] Dr. Frank W. Padelford said.

Freedmen's aid societies of Northern Protestant churches established more than one hundred colleges and secondary institutions. No less a critic than W. E. B. Du Bois has said this effort was

> the finest thing in American history, and one of the few things untainted by
> sordid greed and vainglory. The teachers in these institutions came not to

keep the Negroes in their place, but to raise them out of the defilement of the places where slavery had wallowed them . . . with the best traditions of New England.[6]

Wayland—Richmond—Shaw—Roger Williams—Leland—Augusta Institute—Benedict—Natchez—Alabama Baptist Normal and Theological School—Florida Institute—Kentucky Normal and Industrial Institute—Bishop—Mather—Storer—these names of people and places represent the courage of Baptist women and men that matches the courage of the Civil Rights marchers of our day and that lasted longer.

Literacy had for many years been a crime for slaves and in 1865 stood at 5 percent. In a few decades, 20 percent were literate.

But Northern whites were not the only heroes of this tale. Blacks started schools of their own. The Virginia Seminary, started by black Baptists in 1890, is still located in Lynchburg. But ten other brave efforts died, and these were only the strongest among 147 attempts. Ideas and ideals were not lacking, but money was lacking, and power was lacking.

Blacks also made a strong appeal in the mission-founded organizations for more use of black ideas and black professors. Militant slogans, such as "Colored Teachers for Colored Schools," were met with the bland, unperceptive answer, "The colored people are yet children and need to be taught everything."

But progress did come. Between 1865 and 1870, denominational mission societies operated several hundred elementary schools, aided by the Freedmen's Bureau, and one-fourth of the teachers were black. But the bureau's death at the hands of Northern industrialists and Southern planters—"the lords of the loom and the lords of the lash," Sumner called them—turned most of these schools back to the public school system; and there were no more black teachers.

There was not a single black college president until John Hope became president of Atlanta University in 1907.

Joanna P. Moore, however, was not operating in the best traditions of New England, as Du Bois had put it. She was operating on Island No. 10, with a kind of pioneer down-to-earth Midwest initiative.

Joanna could not get the two women to stop fighting that first day, but she decided later that it was because she only pitied them. "I have learned since that you can never help any one till you love them a little after the way Jesus loved you."[7]

It was bitter cold in the huts she visited, bitter cold in the storeroom where clothing was given out. But despite the hardships, Joanna organized Sunday schools and other meetings. After five months, that camp closed and they were sent to Helena, Arkansas. There the Quakers were beginning work, and Joanna helped in their schools for children. She was glad to work with the Quakers, deeply admiring their commitment, their kindness, and their courtesy.

In another contraband camp near Helena, where nobody was helping, Joanna fixed up a room in a cabin, got the soldiers to make an arbor and seats, nailed a blackboard to a tree, and taught the children and adults to read the Bible. She also led them in singing and praying.

When this camp was sabotaged, Joanna had to go back to Helena. She began to teach the black soldiers who were on guard; she taught ten at a time, many classes a day. Their textbook was the Bible. Soon they began to get new ideas. Evening meetings resulted in the conversion of nearly sixty soldiers.

"I had been a teacher for most of the time among white people for the past fifteen years [she had begun at fourteen, before going to college] but in all that time I never had pupils that learned as fast as some of those boys. They not only memorized, but reasoned; got hold of ideas and expressed them in writing,"[8] Joanna wrote.

She kept in touch with some of them for years. Three of them became faithful ministers of the gospel.

But Joanna wanted also to do something for the women and for the families. Educating teachers and preachers was good, but it did nothing for the present mothers and fathers. She wanted to bring her message into people's homes as a delegate for God—*In Christ's Stead,* as the title of her book suggested. She wanted to *go about* doing good, not to stand still in one place.

She was supported by random gifts until "the organization of our blessed Women's Baptist Home Mission Society . . . when I had the honor of receiving their first commission," she wrote. And the WBHMS also sent "four of the best women that ever lived"[9] to help her.

She started a new project in 1879, the Faith Home for the Aged, to care for homeless old women. She needed help and Kitty Lewis, a seventy-year-old black woman, came to the home and told Joanna: "The Lord showed me a vision that I must come and help you take care of these babies. I am old but I have good health and know how to cook and I want to help you missionaries that the Lord has sent down into this low ground of sorrow. Now I am ready for work."[10]

When the home was established, Joanna turned it over to Negro Baptists and continued her travels. She and her helpers went by train, boat, wagon, and on foot through ten Louisiana parishes, visiting hundreds of homes, organizing Sunday schools, holding temperance meetings, selling Bibles and other books, and *giving* books. Joanna wanted a million dollars to buy books for people. She had a "reading-room craze" and established circulating libraries wherever she could beg, borrow, or steal a little space.

At night she and her fellow workers stayed in black people's houses. These were not always comfortable. "What kind of a bed did you sleep in and what did you have to eat?" people used to ask her. But she answered that one can't focus clearly on two objects at the same time. She was so intent upon the people that other things got only a passing glance.[11] However, she did mention meals of squirrel and cornbread, and she told how they used to run out of the cold little houses to warm up at big bonfires outside.

Sometimes local prejudice was so high that it was dangerous for her and her friends if she stayed with them. However, she always found a place to sleep. Once she was offered a blanket spread over a pile of cotton seed in a railroad station, but she sat up all night. Another time she went to the door of an unwilling white and said, "I am your sister Baptist and I am going to spend the night with you, for you see it is nearly dark."[12]

She was hated by many white people, but the blacks always received her kindly. She visited the associations and helped the black preachers in any way she could. She sat quietly in meetings, making suggestions only when asked, and then humbly and respectfully. "The colored preachers did not seem to care whether I was black or white, male or female," she said.[13]

However, Joanna had a particular mission to women. She not only helped them, but also she trained them to help themselves and to help others by reading the Bible in their neighbors' homes, helping the poor, and caring for the sick. The reports of their giving and doing began to be very impressive—almost too impressive. The men were ruffled. Sister Moore prepared a paper:

> That woman has a work to do in the Christian church no one will deny. All are willing that she work and work hard, but what shall she do? If we can know God's plan, that should settle it; therefore 'to the law and to the

testimony.' In Exodus 15:20, we find Miriam led the women in song as they praise God for his wonderful deliverance. Surely she has a right to sing. After the children of Israel entered Canaan Deborah was appointed as one of the Judges, seemingly with the same power to control as Gideon, Judges 4.[14]

This speech seemed to silence the pastors and encourage the women. But the need to set others to work and to train them preoccupied her. She called for "Training Schools for Mothers," but men as well as women were invited, for Joanna always recognized the man's rights and obligations in the family. Her hope was to give short intensive courses to boarding students, who would then go home as leaders.

Her first effort was in Thibodeaux, and the subjects were "Missionary Work" and the "Training of Children." She could afford a fire only in the schoolroom; so the students had to study wrapped in comforters. They ate a meager Christmas dinner in order to contribute to missions: $2.25 for Africa, $1.25 to the Women's Baptist Home Mission Society.[15]

It was hard to carry the school from place to place, and she tried to establish a permanent center in Baton Rouge. The WBHMS sent her an assistant, Eva Button. Money for the needed building was coming in, and all was bright and promising when she wrote, "All my hopes were shattered and my school destroyed." A notice, decorated with skull and crossbones, ordering that the school be closed, and signed by "The White League," had appeared on the gate.[16]

The teachers were not intimidated, and the students determined to stay, but the next night, a few doors away, a black preacher was so severely beaten by white hoodlums that he almost died. This was too much for the pupils, who packed their trunks and left.

Joanna did not give up; she determined to do it some other way. She decided that a course of study, like the newly developed Chautauqua correspondence course which people could use in their homes, might be her answer. Thus were born the Fireside Schools.

Already, Joanna had established Bible Bands, groups committed to Bible reading and study in their homes and weekly meetings for discussion. Already, in 1885, she had begun to supply them with study helps in the form of a magazine called *Hope*. She had her equipment, and the Fireside Schools soon spread far and wide.

Mrs. Robert Caver, now ninety-one, who lived in Little Rock, Arkansas, writes, "Yes, I remember Sister Joanna Moore—one of the great women of her time; even now her great sacrifice and work live in the hearts of many. Most of the Missionary Societies among Baptist women of colored used her material, depended upon and were inspired by it." [17]

Joanna started things, but she felt people should "do their own." In 1901 she "gave" the Fireside Schools, now administered from Nashville, to a board (selected by herself) of black men and women of different denominations. She believed in ecumenicity as stoutly as she believed in the equality of black and white, of women and men.

She labored on, imaginative, inventive, and daring, intolerant of idleness, of large churches, of emotional money-raising campaigns, and of pastors who "don't cut the food fine enough to feed the children." [18] But she said, "I have differed with many good people, but because we differ I do not need to give them a thrashing. . . ." [19] She never left her work but died on the field, at Selma, Alabama, at the age of eighty-three.

During these same years, 1863 to the early 1900s, many women made notable contributions in institution building. Two of the most dramatic stories are the founding of Spelman College and Mather School.

In 1881, the WABHMS (the Boston Society) voted the establishment of a school for black women and girls in Atlanta, Georgia, and commissioned Sophia B. Packard, their own corresponding secretary, and Harriet E. Giles as teachers. In Atlanta, Rev. Frank Quarles, pastor of Friendship Church, greeted them with the words, "God has sent you." After many hardships during its early development ("we are tired, tired, tired, tired, tired"), Spelman College became well established, and it is now one of the great Atlanta group of colleges.

Mather School, in Beaufort, South Carolina, has been one of the dearest projects of Baptist women. It was founded by Rachel Crane Mather, who on her own opened a day school with a few boarding pupils and was supported by the WABHMS from 1881.

Mather was the only Negro school owned and supported solely by the women, though they helped in many others. It served generations of children and young people who would have had no other opportunity for good schooling or any escape from the rural South Carolina ghettos in which they were born. It went through many phases, beginning as a primary school, advancing to include fifth through ninth grades, and then senior high. By 1932 it had new buildings and had doubled its enrollment, including students from all twelve grades.

In 1950, fire destroyed Coleman Hall, the best building on the campus, and the question arose, "Will Mather ever live again?" But the WABHMS, under Executive Secretary Margaret Wenger, voted to rebuild. This gave Mather a new lease on life and sixteen more years of service. Also in 1950, Eleanor Anderson became the new administrator, the tenth woman to head the school. She came from a career in public school teaching and administration in Iowa and faced a formidable task. It was decided that a combination of high school and junior college would be most useful, but it was tough getting accredited. Dr. Anderson says she spent more time on her knees during the first year there than in all the rest of her life put together. But, she adds, the next twelve years were the most wonderful of her life.

She and her faculty had to take additional courses in order to qualify for the new setup, and the salary schedule had to be upgraded. They received no endowment, but the accrediting committee accepted the Sales House as equivalent to an endowment of $600,000.

The Sales House had been part of Mather's service from the beginning, distributing used clothing sent by the Northern churches to needy students and destitute neighbors. Without charge, it clothed people from the cradle to the grave: expectant mothers stopped on the way to the hospital, and one destitute man was laid out in Sales House graveclothes.

Before long it became clear that it would be wiser to make a small charge. The volume of contributions increased with the realization that they served a double purpose: clothing needy persons and supporting the school. Many people collected clothes for Mather; the women packed the boxes and the men mailed them. Reception of the gifts was described and pictured in magazines. People knew how the buildings looked, how beautifully the students sang, and what became of them. The Sales House came to earn $100 a day.

The administration, especially some of the missionaries, Eleanor Anderson, Aleese Williams, Josie Childs, Eleanor and Mary Opal Crone, and Esther Weinacht, longed to keep standards high, both Christian and academic, and they did. But the times were changing. Public schools were opening to black children. Mailing costs were rising, cutting the profit from the Sales House, and support was not forthcoming from the community. Basically, it was a time and place where a "Negro school" was wrong, unless it could make a unique contribution. Such a contribution for Mather turned out to be a sacrifice which, like all real sacrifices, was really an opportunity.

In 1968, Mather School celebrated its Centennial and simultaneously gave up its resources to two other institutions. Its land was given to the new Beaufort County Branch of South Carolina's trade-school program, and the funds from the sale of its buildings were given to its old companion college, Benedict College, in Columbia, South Carolina.

Benedict College, under the leadership of President Benjamin R. Peyton, is going forward with high standards, full accreditation, and an enrollment of over a thousand students. One hundred of these students are receiving help from the special College Education Achievement Project which trains previously rejected students. Mather's endowment helps in scholarship grants, especially for students from the Beaufort area, its old home. Mather Hall, a fourteen-story dormitory, was built at Benedict in 1970.

With this merger, the twenty-five schools and colleges begun by American Baptist men and women in the post-Civil War period were reduced to seven, now related to the Board of Educational Ministries.

Is beloved Mather gone, its influence dissipated? Part of the answer is expressed by an interview in a Columbia, South Carolina, newspaper,[20] with Edna Smith, the first black woman in South Carolina to pass her bar examination.

One of a poor fatherless family of seven, born in the small town of Yemassee, Edna says she was unusually lucky. "Most people are born and die without ever having a chance to get anywhere. Mostly they just lose hope and give up."

But Edna Smith had a chance to attend "a private school in Beaufort," Mather, of course, and she considers this the turning point in her life.

"I don't want to charge people exorbitant fees. I can get along on a set salary. I don't care about being a judge or moving up the ladder of success," Edna said. "I want to help black people to know what the law is; basically I just want to help people."

# 2

## *The Rope of Love*

Isabel Crawford admitted that she was a terror from childhood. Audacious and curious, at ten she jumped the back fence and sneaked down to the railroad station to find out whether the foreign missionary who had spoken so bravely at church the night before would succeed in not crying when she started off to the foreign field and said good-bye to her children.

But Belle, as she was usually called, did think it was fair to say that she later came to be a *holy* terror. She had been brought up by committed Baptist parents who instilled in her an undying conviction that she was under the guidance of the Holy Spirit.

So after her training at the Baptist Missionary Training School when she was commissioned as a missionary to the Kiowas of Oklahoma, she nearly cried her eyes out, but she went. She said that He drew her and she followed on.

The Indian condition had stirred the conscience of some Christians since the days when Roger Williams protested the enslavement of the Pequots in 1637. At that time no Baptist rallied to his side; they were all too busy fighting for their own freedom.

John Woolman, who felt he had to go to the Indians because he might learn something, was an exception. Most Christians went to teach, rather than to learn.

There was only a handful of early missionaries, whom Charles L. White, first executive secretary of the Home Mission Society, called the "supermen of their generation."

These brave men had no missionary boards to support their work or direct their labors, but with perseverance and tenderness they lovingly led the Indians to the wells of living water, and by their Christian friendship and their superb devotion, averted many misunderstandings and wars, and made possible the normal development of Colonial life.[1]

Missionary boards did spring up, the first in 1809, founded expressly for work among the Tuscaroras of New York. Women began to organize in 1821 to assist in this Indian work, as auxiliaries "to supply the parent organization with funds."

The labors Dr. White speaks of were broad, including vocational training, education, and translation of the Scripture into several Indian languages. This concern did mitigate the disasters of colonialism and supported the hopes of Indians during the period between 1784, when solemn peace treaties were signed with the sachems and warriors of the Six Nations, and 1871, when treaties were declared obsolete. But it was a bleak period for the Indians, at the end of which they had only 140 million acres of the two billion they had formerly possessed. They were soon to lose a great deal more.

Chief Justice John Marshall made judgments favoring the Indians' right to their own land, but President Andrew Jackson merely remarked that John Marshall, having made his decision, was now welcome to try to enforce it. Even Marshall's decisions, based on the Indians' rights not as foreign nations but as domestic dependencies that should be protected by the government, were interpreted to mean that Indians were powerless and it was unnecessary to make treaties with them.

A prevailing view was that neither justice nor wisdom nor humanity should arrest the progress of order and science simply in order that unproductive and barren wastes be reserved for what were considered the "roving barbarians."

The missionaries went along on the Trail of Tears, the Cherokees' flight of sorrow and death from their highly developed homeland before the merciless greed of the advancing frontier. The missionaries held regular religious services, baptizing 170 converts. It was about all they could do when the Reservation System, conceived by missionary Isaac McCoy as an Indian state with political representation and opportunities for education and leadership, was perverted into a reality of seize and shove. The missionaries were committed to "the normal development of Colonial life," but they did recognize the injustices to the Indians and tried to make up for it with the giving of their most precious possessions—their lives and the gospel.

When Isabel Crawford went out to her "blanket" Kiowas, an "uncivilized" tribe as compared to the more settled eastern Indians, she understood the reasons why they were so defiant. "[Satanta] would learn nothing from white men who stole his land, killed his buffalo, and shot the Indians with guns."[2] Satanta, a Kiowa Indian, had escaped hated imprisonment by jumping from the upper balcony of the jail and breaking his neck.

In 1893, only twenty years after the Kiowas had been subdued, Belle Crawford arrived at the Kiowa settlement of Elk Creek, where other missionaries, including the lovely Maryetta Reeside, were already at work. Belle had been deaf from childhood, but she made a virtue of that by quickly learning the Indian sign language.

"Then the people of Saddle Mountain invited me to come over there and I went," she records.

They were impressed by her courage, a woman alone, coming to give them the Jesus way. She told them of the new road the Holy Spirit would show them; she shared their lives, their leaky tents, and their pilgrimage to Rainy Mountain to get the government allotment; and she shared their fury when white gamblers cheated them out of it. But she did it all "with her hand over her mouth."[3] Keeping quiet was her duty, but it went against the grain.

Then she learned that her mother had died. The Indians heard what had happened, and the oldest Indian, the one who had come to Elk Creek to ask her to come to Saddle Mountain, embraced her and prayed: "O Great Spirit, our leetle Jesus woman has lost her mother, and her heart is all broken to pieces. Gather it together again and put it back strong. You have given her to us now, and we will take the best care of her we know how."[4]   By expressing their sympathy in their own touching way, they opened her eyes to the real merit of "heart culture."

Isabel lived in a tent until Lucius Aitsan and his wife invited her to share their cottage. Belle found all the Kiowas except Lucius quite indifferent to the idea of a church. But he was an important exception, picking up new ideas readily and putting them into practice. Using his two-year-old daughter as an object lesson, he gave almost all her birthday money to start a building fund. The Kiowas were so impressed with his generosity that they began to contribute, and by 1903, with help from the WABHMS, they were able to build a church.

The concept of church as a *building* was hard to put across to the Indians, but the missionaries, feeling it their obligation, managed to do so. Across woodland and prairie and desert, and up the long coast of California, the missionaries fixed up whatever building they found and put up whatever structure they could.

Professor Almon C. Bacone wanted 160 acres near Muskogee,

Oklahoma, in order to build a college for the Indians. However, he didn't get it from the Creek Council until a member of the council, who was also a Baptist minister, had argued all night, telling the Creeks that people would think they were opposed to education if they didn't give in.

Learning to give to others was, to the missionaries, a prime essential in becoming a Christian. And of course the greatest gift was the gospel. The Jesus road was explained:

> Jesus left word for all who walked his road to tell other people the Good News. Some gave money to help and some went out to explain about the Jesus Road, but all of the Christians prayed. . . . We can . . . give money to send the Gospel to another tribe.[5]

Thus Isabel, like all the others, organized a missionary society (not for women only) and called it "God's Light upon the Mountain." The missionary gift box was set out beside the building fund box. This stimulated the WABHMS, and in 1901 "God's Sunlight" mission was founded for the Hopis at Second Mesa, Arizona. Belle described this event in her picturesque Crawford-Indian, "God's Light upon a Mountain has borned a papoose!"[6]

The Indians responded, "My heart feels like stretched."

More and more women missionaries went to the Indian field. It had early become clear that schools alone could do little to change family life and Indian culture. President Grant had instituted a "Peace Policy," also known as the "Quaker Policy," encouraging missionaries to undertake the acculturation of the Indians, and it was clear that women were needed to speak to women, to teach cleanliness, godliness, and child care.

Women's ministry to the Indian women involved a wide variety of tasks, from carrying sewing machines and simple medicines across the wilderness to alternating with the ministers in preaching. Abigail Johnson directed the building of the Hopi church and reconstructed an old organ. But men generally determined policy, and women generally accepted the rule of obedience.

Not always. The "holy terror," guided by the spirit, staged a revolt.

In 1905, the "Blanket Indian Association" passed a resolution accusing the Saddle Mountain Church and its missionary of having walked on a crooked road. The church was denounced from the pulpit, reported to headquarters, and threatened with expulsion from the association.

On Communion Sunday, when the nearest minister was not able to follow the usual practice of coming to administer the ordinance, Miss Crawford had recommended that Lucius Aitsan do it. The church had voted in the affirmative.

"The vote was perfectly unanimous and the service was conducted with so much feeling that every heart overflowed and tears sparkled in many eyes. Never once did we dream of trouble. In obeying the command of the Master we supposed that everyone interested would rejoice. . . ."[7]

Miss Crawford was convinced that the individual church under the guidance of the Holy Spirit was autonomous. However, the association felt that only "Jesus men" could administer Communion.

In an effort to adjudicate the matter, Miss Mary Burdette and Mrs. R. R. Donnelley came from WABHMS headquarters. They were joined by Dr. A. B. Rairden of the ABHMS, but the difference of view remained. The Indians were bewildered.

This, in fact, became the major issue to be decided. While many of the theologians of the denomination wrote to support Miss Crawford, some of them thought she should sacrifice her point for the sake of harmony. However, Dr. Charles E. Stanton, district superintendent of the ABHMS from 1912–1919, after citing various authorities in her favor, wrote:

> I would be sorry to see you lay down the management of the work at Saddle Mountain. You could hardly, however, recede from the stand you have taken without injuring your influence. The Indians would say, "If Miss Crawford is mistaken about this road, she may be about others also." Their confidence in you would be shaken. You can retire gloriously as it is, true to your principles and strong in the feeling that you are right.[8]

He went on to suggest that she might well ask for ordination herself, since she was well qualified. But Isabel was not up to that degree of feminism. She commented, "It is bad enough to be called an old maid, but to be called a Reverend Old Maid would finish me in 24 hours!"[9] (Later, women missionaries to the Indians, such as Ioleta McElhaney, were ordained.)

Isabel could not bear to prolong the Indians' pain at this dispute among those who had come to show them the way. She left the church in the hands of Lucius Aitsan, admonishing the church members to remember above all to love one another, and that when the new pastor came, they ought not to kick him!

Isabel Crawford traveled about the country, speaking about the Kiowas and escorting them to meetings and conventions. Her books were candid and readable. Her experiences and point of view exerted a great deal of influence throughout the denomination.

During this period in the early nineteen hundreds, countless sacrifices and adjustments were being made by other vigorous women, working competently along with the men. Many small churches were built in the wilderness, and many small groups of people were wrested away from the remains of tribal religions and culture or were rescued from utter deprivation.

The missionaries spent fifty years of continuous and largely happy toil. At various places, these efforts bloomed and gave increase. Will Rogers is quoted in Bacone records as having said, when he visited there, "Bacone College has provided three times as many Indian leaders as all the government millions of dollars have done." After serving as an exclusively Indian college for many years, Bacone has opened its doors to all races and strengthened its board by becoming community oriented. Dorothy Bucklin was primarily responsible for the latter project while she was associate executive secretary of the ABHMS and a Bacone College board member.

Women have always been active on the Bacone faculty and staff as they have been in the Murrow Home for Children, located on the same campus. Examples are Ioleta Hunt McElhaney, a notable Indian teacher, administrator, and writer, well-known throughout the denomination; and Annette Anderson, a Mono Indian, a member of the Baptist church, who grew up in a Christian home, and who now carries top responsibility for the Indian work in the denomination. Her appointment fulfilled recommendations made in an evaluation of Indian work done by the Board of National Ministries in 1972.

This evaluation made it clear that though Indian churches had become a beloved part of our denomination and small churches and centers still carry on their work in several states, notably Oklahoma, Arizona, Nevada, and Montana, the church had not adequately prepared Indian leadership to deal with their own problems. At some points (notably at the time of Termination,[10] in the 1950s) the church had challenged unjust government policies, but in general had not come to grips with the issues and the systems which were affecting Indian people and which kept them from being whole persons in a position to control their own destiny.

The majority of the 800,000 Indians in this country today lead marginal lives. The average family income of Indians on reservations is about $1,500 a year. Life expectancy is nearly one-third shorter than the national average. The average educational level for all Indians under federal supervision is five school years. Only $18 a child is allotted for books and supplies for Indian children compared to $40 for a white child. The tuberculosis rate among Indians exceeds the national rate by 500 percent. Professional services, medical care, and justice before the law are for Indians all but nonexistent.

"In eastern Oklahoma," stated a Ponca Indian, Clyde Warrior, "we have a system of peonage. . . . The life of most Oklahoma Indians is very, very bad, the sickest, poorest people in the country." [11]

In view of all this, new proposals have been made, not to abandon what the past produced, but to consolidate and strengthen viable units, while channeling our greatest efforts through inter-denominational projects to strengthen the Indian community itself. For example, the Baptists are collaborating with the Cook Christian Training School in Tempe, Arizona, to prepare and provide more Indian leadership.

The creation of an Indian Caucus within the Board of National Ministries provides promise of fuller use of peculiarly Indian insights which are urgently needed.

The image of the "rope of love" which drew the Indians out of their defeat and deprivation into the haven of Christianity was used by Isabel Crawford in her paraphrase of the Twenty-third Psalm for the Kiowas:

> He throws out to me a rope. The name of the rope is "Love." He draws me and draws me and draws me to where the grass is green and the water not dangerous. And I eat and drink and lie down satisfied. [12]

But in some cases it may have become a rope that bound and limited Indian initiative. Now we hope for something different—not that we relinquish the bond between us, but that we hold onto one end only, hoping the Indians will take a firm grip on the other. It may be a tug of war, but not a fight.

But we must not let go of our end. Vine Deloria, Jr., in his powerful *We Talk, You Listen,* decries liberal interference and asks liberals to "leave us alone." But he is not saying "leave us alone" to all whites.

> Many of these people have offered specific technical skills, have raised funds for us, sponsored events so that we can present our message, and done yeoman volunteer work on behalf of various Indian causes. We will need that type of assistance for some time to come. [13]

# 3

# Praying on the Run

"There's Setzie!"

A whisper, a rustle, and whatever the meeting, conference, or convention, it was delightfully disrupted, as the stocky figure appeared and the round, cheerful face broadcast smiles for everyone—that is, everyone but an audacious iconoclast who might defy her, flout her ideals, or threaten her relationship with her precious children.

That was Setzie—Mary Setzekorn, the "mother" of about a hundred Alaskan children: Aleut children, or rather, Aleut-Russian, Aleut-Japanese, Aleut-Norwegian, Aleut-American, or Aleut-hyphenated-anything-else that reflected the periodic invasions suffered by this remote, magnetic, half-frozen land. Such children have been part of Alaska's history for the last two hundred years.

The United States bought Alaska from the Russians in 1867, and ten years later the Baptists were being urged to develop a mission on Kodiak Island. The need for responsible leadership there was acute.

Dr. Sheldon Jackson, U.S. Commissioner for Education in Alaska, wrote in the *North Star* for April, 1891, that the entire economy of Alaska had been destroyed by the rapacious U.S. industries which devastated the whale population, then the walrus, the salmon, and the reindeer. Villages were abandoned; people were starving; and children were destitute.

"We dare hesitate no longer," wrote Dr. and Mrs. R. E. Roscoe. Dr. Roscoe was employed as a government teacher in Kodiak. "To do our work here, we must have not only a school but a home for the children."

There had been a surplus population of children ever since 1741 when fur traders and hunters from eastern Siberia had invaded the Bering Sea. Greedy, tough, and unscrupulous, they stripped the Aleutians by the end of the 1750s, plundering sea otter, black fox, cross fox, red fox, and blue fox and destroying people and villages along the way. They hit Kodiak (named for the Koniags, Alaska's early people) in 1763. The Russians started consolidating their holdings by building a village on the island in 1792, and they brought in the Orthodox Church in 1796. There was by now a substantial population of mixed-blood orphans, and some effort was made to start schools and hospitals.

When the American Military Occupation took over, all such work dwindled away, and there was "nothing but rum and ruin" for ten years. Mrs. Roscoe made sure the Woman's American Baptist Home Mission Society knew all about the conditions on Kodiak Island, and they commissioned her as their missionary in 1886. She kept on writing, and in 1891 they voted to build an orphanage across the bay on Woody Island.

The project was presented persuasively to the home churches by Mrs. James McWhinnie. The children contributed cards called "planks and shingles," each costing one dollar. By 1892, $4,000 had been raised to buy lumber, but the lumber had to be shipped up from San Francisco; and the building had to rise under the hostile glare of the Russian Orthodox Church. But at last, in 1893, the Roscoes were able to move in. The building wasn't quite completed, but they could not wait any longer. They were eager to open its shelter to the needy children.

Both the urgency of the need and the difficulty of operating at such a formidable distance have characterized the work at Kodiak Baptist Children's Home and all other Baptist work in Alaska since the beginning. But the call, when heard, has proved irresistible to generations of workers. The contrasts of Kodiak Island, with its rugged mountains rising out of the sea, its spruce-covered hills, its surprisingly mild climate interspersed with howling gales, its plentiful sea life and richness of grass, flowers, and berries, appeal to the romantic and adventurous; and its human need cries out to the compassionate.

When Mary Setzekorn graduated from Baptist Missionary Training School (BMTS) in 1938, she heard the trumpets that had sounded for the Roscoes, Miss Carrie Currant, Miss Lou Goodchild, the Faordorffs, the Coes, the Learns, and the Rickmans before her. The Lord had called her to Kodiak, and she was qualified (a registered nurse) and eager.

Then she had her final physical. She could not be considered for such an appointment. Her heart was too bad. It was out of the question for a woman in her condition to go to Kodiak where the mail boat called only once a week, and an ill person would be dangerously stranded. Besides, the work was too hard. The missionary there had to be a domestic servant in the uncompromising style of the pioneers.

But Setzie wouldn't give up.

"I'll get my family to agree not to hold you responsible if anything happens to me," she suggested. "Just pay my way up there, that's all I ask!" [1]

There was no resisting her. She went as a volunteer in 1939 but in 1940 was hired at the princely salary of $1260, plus living expenses. She was sent to Baker Cottage, in Ouzinkie, Spruce Island; it was a two-story frame building, combining the functions of a children's home and a Christian center for the village of about three hundred native Alaskans. The natives made their living by fishing, hunting, and trapping in the winter and by working at the cannery from June to September. The arrival of a nurse in the village caused general rejoicing.

But Mary wasn't just a nurse. She was everything. She worked in the garden, did the laundry, baked bread, and mended; she taught and took care of the children. In that she gloried. She spoiled the children and monopolized them. She accepted help from her fellow workers with good grace, but all the same, the children were all hers.

Mary was happy and, despite the bad prognosis, appeared to keep healthy and buxom; not only buxom, but hippy.

"Well, there's just one satisfaction about that," she said, as she climbed a perilous ladder, "I'm balanced, fore and aft!"

Setzie wasn't always easy to work with or to direct; she was too passionately devoted to be willing to put up with anything she considered stupid or unnecessary. One worker arrived who believed in two-hour devotions every day. Mary was fit to be tied.

"*I* pray as I run!" she said. The meditating missionary didn't last long. But Mary did.

In the words of one fellow worker, "Mary was as nearly completely committed as anyone, ever."

Another worker said, "She turned out wonderful young men and women."

Setzie served as Public Health Nurse during World War II; she was flown by the navy to other islands. But she did this only out of necessity, writing once, "To be the *laundress* for the Kodiak Baptist Mission presents a far greater challenge to me than to be the Alaskan

Field Service Nurse for the whole of Kodiak Island. Please remember this when you start the September Kodiak Checker Game. My prayers are with you through it all."[2] (Her prayers and her caveats as well!)

She wrote almost with zest about whooping cough, flu, and how Ralph fell and injured his chin, and she added, "Then we entertained the mumps."

In 1953 she wrote about vacation church school, about day camp, church youth camp, and about riding in the sixtieth anniversary float, in which the children were dressed as flowers, and the Kodiak Mission float won first prize.

Setzie wrote about the *Evangel* trip on the Fourth of July. The *Evangel* was a 38-foot motor boat, the hull of which had been bought by the WABHMS from the navy. The superstructure was built by Glenn Chandler, and in this boat he and his wife plied through a dozen villages on the Kodiak Islands. The Norman Smiths took it over later, anchoring it for the winter in Larson Bay. In 1960, because the boat was old and flying had become so much more practicable, it was turned over to the Sea Scouts.

Setzie made, from time to time, strong recommendations. "We need a man at Baker Cottage—such a lot of heavy work to be done, like taking the drain down to the sea." "We need a washer; Baker Cottage should be moved to Kodiak." "I don't care for this unit administration."

But she also wrote, "I still do not feel any urgent need of furlough."[3]

She stayed until 1958, and soon after that she was appointed to the Christian Center at Billings, Montana. They had trouble with her there, too. They gave her an air conditioner to help her through the boiling summer, and she had it installed in the children's room!

John and Virginia Winter went to Kodiak in 1943, arriving on a ship that had to penetrate an antisubmarine net. The mission home, for the second time, had been destroyed by fire and had been reconstructed on the cottage plan, as suggested by Miss Alice Brimson, then secretary of the Woman's American Baptist Home Mission Society. Each cottage was built to accommodate up to fourteen children, with a foster mom and pop to bring them up. Virginia Winter, who was a mom, had to bake ten loaves of bread three times a week, and John Winter, who was a pop, was also plumber, purchasing agent, dispensing clerk, inventory master, bookkeeper and report-writer, as well as superintendent of the mission. The Winters remained in Kodiak almost three years, at which time illness forced their return to the States.

The William Stones arrived in 1946, devoting twenty-four years of productive labor to the management of the mission.

Cattle is raised by the Children's Home to supply a measure of self-support; and housekeeping, cooking, and maintenance skills are taught the children as they share work with their foster parents. Even though the background of children and foster parents is so different—the newcomers are sometimes frightened by the uncompromising cleanliness and formal manners—there usually develops a very warm and wonderful feeling in the homes, and the children find real and lasting homelife relationships.

The plant has gradually developed, and modern conveniences have been supplied, but the self-reliant style continues. And despite the hardships, the isolation, the oppressiveness of the long winter nights, the wind, the heavy rainfall, the huge bears lurking in the hills, the noise of the storms, and the fatigue, the foster parents find real relationships, too, and a kind of fascination hard to describe. Home economics, electronic engineering, elementary education, and music are taught by recent recruits, a hardy and talented lot with a variety of education and experience in social work, farming, carpentry, plumbing, church work, meatcutting, and many sidelines. They can use it all.

The mission work in Alaska spread from its beginnings on Kodiak and Woody Islands to Anchorage and Cordova, adapting to the needs that were found with what resources it could muster. It also contributed to the social development of Alaska, introducing ideas and helping upgrade standards.

The latest of these creative adaptations is known as the Alaska Children's Services. It was formed in Anchorage in 1970, through the merging of the Lutheran Youth Center, the United Methodist Jesse Lee Home (for children with behavior problems), and the Anchorage Children's Christian Home. The Anchorage Children's Christian Home included the emergency center and girls' group home, Colletti House, developed by John and Dorothy Molletti.

In addition to carrying on the original functions, the merged institutions have started five new projects. Two of them, the Center for Children and Parents and North Star House, have cooperative connections with the American Baptist Churches.

The Center for Children and Parents approaches the needs of family life comprehensively. It provides preschool day-care and social services to children in their own homes. It also provides family counseling for couples individually as well as in seminars, whichever is needed. This service includes counseling on such topics as budgeting, infant care, family-life enrichment, and birth control. The center also recruits, trains, and licenses foster families.

North Star House serves adolescent boys, receiving boys from several other agencies of Alaska Children's Services. It provides a warm living situation while the boys are in transition from special care to life in the larger community.

Alaska is still far away, but not as far as it was. Volunteers sent by the American Baptist National Ministries' Office of Volunteer Services are now appearing every summer to work at Kodiak and Anchorage, some of whom are going back as regular workers.

The services begun in 1893 by the women are still operating. Young couples now run the cottages where Mary Setzekorn worked, and there is "a man to take the drain down to the sea."

The Alaska Children's Services intend to do everything they can to insure an adequate upbringing for Alaska's children by giving them temporary care during emergencies and by trying to figure out how to solve the problems that cause the emergencies.

# 4

# *The Road from Castle Garden*

Castle Garden was an abandoned fort at the south end of New York City that was for many years used as a reception center for immigrants from Europe. The collection place for immigrants was transferred to Ellis Island in 1890 when the federal government took charge.

But even before this, missionaries had been provided by the Women's Baptist Home Mission Society to welcome and help the newcomers. Extracts from their letters give some feeling of the situation. In Mary Burdette's publication, *Home Missions Lessons,*[1] we find two letters, one from Maria Rapp and the other from Mary Melby.

> Last week we found a Bohemian mother with four little children, the eldest was about four years old, the next two were twins, about seventeen months old, but not yet able to walk, and the youngest was a babe about two months old. She wanted to go to Pittsburgh to see the husband. They had their tickets paid for but wanted food. After they were provided with bread and coffee you would have enjoyed the sight of those little ones and their happy mother. During the afternoon Miss Melby and myself bought a pair of woolen stockings for one of the twins whose little bare feet looked so cold, and for the eldest girl a shawl, it had been such a cold day; how happy the mother looked. Then we added a Bohemian testament which she promised to read. . . . Among so many different people and in such circumstances, we find use for everything we learned while in the Training School.

Mary Melby wrote:

> At Castle Garden we could not always care for the helpless girls and women because of the privileges granted to the runners. But on Ellis Island these are kept out and we can do all that our time and means permit. But the runners are not at a great distance; they stay outside and every immigrant that comes out is picked up and dragged away; sometimes they quarrel among themselves and frighten the poor people back to the building.

The ambiguous nature of America's attitude toward immigrants is apparent in this passage and in other contemporary Baptist writings. Rev. J. C. Grimmell, general secretary of the German Baptist Conference in 1883, observed: "The vast majority come with motives of peaceful interest—to be free, to have a home of their own, to be on an equality with the men around them. Nine out of every ten immigrants that step upon the plank carry a bundle or a baby. Not one in four million wears a crown or has one safely packed in a trunk or valise. . . ."[2]

But on the other hand, a dean of the Divinity School of Chicago University describes the steadily increasing immigrants of the 1880s and 1890s thus:

> The old world can spare two million people a year and not decrease her population. As a matter of fact, she is sparing half a million a year, mostly from southern Europe—the worst dregs we have ever taken in. . . . They pour in upon us the degradation and wretchedness of the peasantry of Europe; the low-born and the low-bred, a mixed multitude of paupers and criminals, ignorant, clannish, sullen, vicious, ripe for revolution. . . .[3]

Only the "runners" were wholeheartedly eager to claim the newcomers, to sign them up as low-cost laborers, and to cram them into the worsening slums where they would be at the mercy of industries that required vast pools of cheap labor.

But the Christians of America, despite their bewilderment and apprehension about "skeptics and scoffers, antagonistic toward our public school systems, their attitude in favor of intoxicating beverages, and their open disregard of the Sabbath,"[4] were constrained to move beyond prejudice. The incoming multitudes "awakened the most intense solicitude in every discerning mind or Christian heart. . . . The disciple of Jesus must leave the ninety and nine and go forth after the lost."[5]

The ABHMS began its work in 1836 among the Welsh immigrants and extended it in the following years to Germans, Scandinavians, and French. The Michigan women formed their Woman's Baptist Home Mission Society in 1873 largely to respond to this need. The Chicago and New York societies included the "heathen immigrants" in their stated responsibility, and began by sending Elizabeth Johnson in 1870 to work among the Scandinavians of the Northwest. Soon women were working among Germans, Bohemians, and Hungarians.

The road from Castle Garden led everywhere, not just to crowded city streets or enclaves of bewildered foreigners. The women's societies recognized the needs of isolated frontier women and also felt a conviction that the women could help themselves by supporting the struggling new state conventions. They decided the women should assume the responsibility of collecting the mission apportionment each church was supposed to contribute.

After this move to try to undergird the new structures of the western church, the women's societies also sent their emissaries to start new work. Women went to the mill community of Columbia, South Carolina, to the mining camps of Carbon and Juab in Utah, and to the mining settlements of West Virginia. Miss Minnie A. Matthews and Miss Alice Matthews became experts in service to mining communities. In 1913 in Colorado, women tried to help people through the emergencies of the coal strike. In New Mexico and Arizona, in Denver and Pueblo, women opened schools and Christian Centers for Mexican immigrants.

The road from Castle Garden also led to Utah, where the women were anxious to follow immigrants whose way to the United States had been paid by the Mormons. Many thought that the Mormons exploited them for their labor and degraded them by polygamy.

It was probably the Christian Centers that became the most effective institutional expression of the women's concern for the immigrants. The centers were a new kind of project, modeled after the home, and were not already monopolized by men. The local church usually sponsored the work, and volunteers staffed it. When the need for institutionalizing it was seen, women were entrenched, ready for joint responsibility.

The Christian Center movement rose in the decade between 1910 and 1920. The four earliest centers with which the women's societies cooperated were of several styles. The Japanese Women's Home of Seattle was founded in 1905 to provide a specific service to a particular nationality. The Mission House for Negroes, opened in Brooklyn in 1910, was the result of one woman's interest and lasted only five years, which was characteristic of the Christian Centers operating exclusively for blacks under white auspices. A work begun in 1911 in Brooklyn at the Italian Baptist Church of the Transfiguration prospered so well that it emerged into self-sufficiency; the Italian centers in Newark, Camden, Philadelphia, Providence, and New York were generally closely sponsored by churches, and they carried on strong work until the assimilation of Italians was far progressed. Aiken Christian Center, opened in Chicago in 1911, was typical of the largest category of Christian Centers, serving multinational, largely white communities.

Aiken began in a church building, from which the congregation had "moved on," and was staffed by volunteers. In 1914 two women were called by the Woman's Home Mission Society and developed a large work centering on religious services, majoring in children. *Fifty Golden Years,* written by Mrs. Orrin Judd, Sr., former president of the WABHMS Board, tells us that in 1927 the Aiken Daily Vacation Bible School held the world's attendance record for the eleventh consecutive year: 600 boys and 785 girls. The regular staff and boys' worker and assistant were supplemented by volunteers, all members of the local constituency.

Brooks House, founded by the ABHMS in Hammond, Indiana, was dedicated September 14, 1919, the day of the Calumet riots. Its clinic was baptized by the giving of emergency care to five wounded strikers. Katherine House, another Indiana Christian Center, opened the same year by the WABHMS, served Hungarian, Polish, Rumanian, and Mexican laborers. In Kansas City, Dayton, Pittsburgh, Omaha, Weirton, Boston, Chicago, Buffalo, Detroit, and Dearborn, such havens welcomed, taught, comforted, and encouraged the stranger. Some Christian Centers were founded by the ABHMS and the WABHMS together, some separately, but soon all were run jointly, except for the appointment of missionaries.

Luella Adams Killiam Funk tells of her work at the Rankin Mission, Pittsburgh, when its work among Slavic and Magyar people had been going on in a chapel for several years.[6]

I'd come straight from the country to Chicago, and I wanted to go to Cuba or Puerto Rico, but Mrs. Westfall, executive secretary of the WABHMS, told me I should go to Pittsburgh. I couldn't stand the place! Those dirty houses! But my father opposed my going, so of course I couldn't give up.

It was a time of great immigration. Hundreds of new people were arriving, absolutely destitute; pretty soon there were ten thousand of them, hired at wages they couldn't live on. There were strikes [no unions, of course], and the mill owners were very unfair. They brought in Mexicans to break the strike, and they brought Negroes on barges and put them in the mill where they slept on the floor and the mill people fed them. When the strike was over, those Negroes didn't want to go South, and some stayed in Rankin. Those there at first were descended from freedmen.

It was really a revolution, the state constabulary riding black stallions that were so well trained they could control and terrorize the crowd. The people were having to work twelve hours a day, you see—terrible conditions.

Then I got a dream. We needed something better than that little old mission. First I got rid of the privy. The kids were running to it through all the meetings, disturbing everybody. Then I talked to the Pittsburgh people and got volunteers, Croatians, Serbs, Croats, Hungarians, Italians, and many from the English churches. I wanted it international. Mrs. Paulinyi helped me, you know; she was a Hungarian with command of five Slavic languages, and she was heroic in many ways.

Finally I got the Association and the State and Boards to commit themselves to the idea of a Christian Center. I used to write about it, articles for *Missions Magazine,* on a little old Oliver typewriter, till 3 A.M. That was in 1919 or 1920.

Then we got smart—Charles Brooks, Mrs. Westfall, and I—and got me on the program for the Convention, meeting in Denver. I put it over! Both boards voted to back the project.

We had to buy extra lots and collect rents on the buildings there until we could build. The first plans were terrible; I cried when I saw them! The gym on the fifth floor, the workers' rooms on the fourth right under it! The new plans called for more space. We needed $5,000 to buy extra lots. I helped them to raise the money and to interest the people in the churches.

Once I went to a home where a maid ushered me in to where a nice old gentleman sat. I told about the sick babies and mothers and the young people who needed guidance. Afterward, the city secretary received a feebly penned letter from the old gentleman promising us $2,000. He died a week later.

The old chapel had to be torn down. The contractor started to rip off the old clapboards, and the women came and begged and fought for the wood and tore down the building in less than a day.

While the new one was being built, we had to rent an old corner-store front room. We fixed it up the best we could, hung nice curtains, and used it one year while waiting for the real building. I used to make it as lovely as possible on Saturday night, but the first Sunday morning I went in and found a stream running clear through it—moonshine!

"Miss Adams!" the church members cried, "What are you doing?" The moonshiners fled.

There was so little room we had to do it in sections, meeting small groups. We got very close to some of the young people in that little tiny room. I felt like a mother to all those girls. Their mothers appreciated it and wanted me to tell the girls the facts of life. We went into the old mission in the chilly evening, and were talking—when the floor caught on fire! The boys had crawled underneath to listen.

In October, 1922, the cornerstone was laid. It was a lovely building. We had two more workers now, and we all lived in a nice apartment in the Center, with a communal living room, nicely carpeted, and Haviland dishes. We had many volunteers there, partly through the World Wide Guild, and from the many young men and even women who were coming up from the South from Clemson and Furman. Several of them became missionaries and ministers. I remember one handsome boy named Wade Bryant.

People bought membership tickets for twenty-five cents, and there were around eight hundred. Membership allowed them to use the showers; there was no water then in most of the houses except the sink. They needed Americanization classes; they needed cooking and sewing. There was no high school for them to go to. We got sewing machines; and we also taught piano lessons and singing. The boys' worker used to have almost one hundred on Saturday for showers and basketball. I saw my first basketball played there, and I couldn't keep out of the balcony at night, watching!

Our staff included an administrator and a stenographer now. We had many activities—like a mandolin club. German refugees from the Hitler regime came to us, cultured people who had no money.

I worked hard at Rankin, but I felt limited educationally. BMTS hadn't prepared me for all I met there. I felt I needed more college; so I went to the West End Christian Center at Boston. At first I regretted my decision, feeling the old work needed me; but it was a blessed time, too.

Luella went on to ever-expanding realms, reveling in her college courses, taking a trip to Europe that included a visit to the Christian Center at West Ham, London. She returned to do a speaking tour and then was offered jobs in the New York office and at Berkeley. She decided on the latter, taking her master's degree at Berkeley Baptist Divinity School while serving there as dean of women. Later she married John Killiam of the Publication Society and shared his work as colporteur in the West. She was for two years chairman of the National Committee on Women's Work, served a term as eastern vice-president of WABHMS, and made many visits to the mission fields.

But her work at Rankin stands alone, because of its deep and continuing influence through those served.

She says: "I told you about the Negroes who stayed. One who came to the Center when we began to admit Negroes [one day a week] was Dorothy Height. I remember her so well with her cute little pigtails. That Negro day was the jolliest day of the week!"

Dorothy Height remembers that day, too. Rankin was on her line of march, near home and across the street from Immanuel Baptist Church. It was natural for her to drop in and take part sometimes, and when she was eleven, she offered to help with the Day-Care Center. "I like to tell Bible stories," she told Miss Adams. One day when she was holding a group of Hungarian and Croatian children spellbound, two distinguished visitors dropped in and listened. Although she didn't know then who they were, they later played a very important role in her life.

One Thursday Dorothy was watching a basketball game at Rankin when her attention was caught by a sign posted on the gymnasium wall:

> WOULD YOU LIKE TO GO TO COLLEGE? If so, enter the
> Oratorical Contest on the Constitution of the U.S., sponsored
> by the Elks of the World.

Dorothy was a Depression child; there had seemed no way to realize her ambition to go to college. Maybe this was it! She entered the contest, won it, and was on her way. She went to New York University. Field work assignments were hard to come by—it was still Depression time—and what she wanted was to work at the Brownsville Community Center, but there was no money for her salary. A possible benefactor was approached and, on learning who the recipient would be, was delighted to provide what was needed. She was Mrs. Orrin Judd, Sr.—one of the women who had seen young Dorothy teach the children at Rankin!

A bare outline of Dorothy Height's achievements and honors would take many pages. As director of the Center for Racial Justice of the YWCA of the U.S.A., she has done outstanding leadership training and interracial education. As national president of the National Council of Negro Women, Inc. (concurrently), she has led in combating malnutrition, bad housing, inferior education, and other problems that attack the poor. Recognition of her accomplishments includes appointment to innumerable national boards and commissions, and her selection as Woman of the Year, in 1973, by the *Ladies' Home Journal.*

On July 10, 1974, the Secretary of Interior, the Director of the National Park Service, and Dr. Dorothy Height sent out invitations for the dedication of a memorial to Mary McLeod Bethune, the illustrious founder of the National Council of Negro Women, whom Dorothy Height succeeded as president, and the first black American, or woman, to be so honored. On the invitation was included part of Mrs. Bethune's last will and testament. Perhaps Rankin and the WABHMS have been trying to make the same sort of gifts.

> I Leave You Love—I Leave You Hope—I Leave You the Challenge of Developing Confidence in One Another—I Leave You a Thirst for Education—I Leave You a Respect for the Use of Power—I Leave You Faith—I Leave You Racial Dignity—I Leave You a Desire to Live Harmoniously with Your Fellowman—I Leave You, Finally, a Responsibility to our Young People.

# 5

## A Right to Their Footing

The Chinese wife, when scolded, said: "I am not your servant; I came to you by betrothal; six ceremonies were duly performed. I have a right to my footing."[1]

With this story, Dong Gong, in an article in the *Home Mission Monthly* for 1892, illustrates the position of the Chinese immigrants who heard in 1849 of the opportunity to work in the gold fields in the United States, and who came in large numbers, about 22,000 altogether, mostly under the auspices of the labor companies. In the hope of riches (25 cents a day for a laborer, as much as the boss earned in China) they sailed hopefully to Kam San. However, their only welcome, after the first curiosity faded, was abuse.

Though the Chinese had supplied a great need in the mining industry after the first rush of feverish goldseekers ebbed, and had also been an indispensable labor source as farmers, mill builders, ditchdiggers, and the main laborers on the railways across the mountains and over the plains, they worked for small wages and were considered unfair competitors by the later flood of American and foreign laborers who poured into California. The missionary observers noted the conflict of interests between protection of American natives and response to universal human need.

The Board of the Baptist State Convention of California decreed: "It having been found that the work of women among the Chinese has been greatly blessed, and there being about 1,400 Chinese families in San Francisco, and 3,000 children of school age, but who are not admitted by the public schools, it is suggested that the Woman's Baptist Home Mission Society should be invited to cooperate in the mission."[2]

Mrs. J. N. Crouse, president of the Society, agreed, and in 1884 the women undertook the support of Mrs. J. L. Sanford, the only woman missionary in San Francisco who spoke Chinese. This helped reconstruct a work that had been almost routed.

The Home Mission Society, impoverished by the crash of 1873 and under criticism from its own churches, had suspended the mission to the Chinese in 1879. In 1880 they hoped that "a healthy reaction [had] set in," but the problems were not over. In 1885 there were outbreaks in which scores of Chinese were massacred and their property destroyed in Rock Springs, Wyoming Territory, and in Seattle and Takoma, Washington Territory. In 1890, the Chinese were confined by the Education Supervisors to San Francisco's Chinatown. And though the California Baptist Convention protested, even among them there was some division as to whether "Chinese who had evidently been converted by the grace of God should be allowed to join a church of white people."[3]

A law was passed in 1892 requiring every Chinese, on pain of arrest, imprisonment, or deportation, to carry a certificate of residence. Restrictive immigration laws were passed, repealed, and passed again.

The Mission Societies were indignant about injustices to the Chinese and thought their duty included trying to secure helpful legislation, as well as giving the gospel.

This mission to the Chinese in the United States was not only for their sakes. The relationship between the Christian mission in China and the mission to the Chinese in the United States was always kept in mind. The Sacramento conversion of Wong Min, who came to be known as the Chinese Luther for his splendid work in Canton, was an example of what was hoped for: To send many Chinese who had become Christians in the United States back to China to witness to their fellow countrymen. Nearly two thousand persons now belonged to Baptist churches in China, but that was not enough. Of all the Lord's vineyards, as David Halbersham writes in *The Best and the Brightest,* China was perhaps the best loved.

There was much coming and going between the United States and China. Chinese pastors served in the U.S.A. and then went back to China, and pastors of China came out of China to the United States to stay. The missionaries who could speak Chinese were in great demand on both shores. Nellie Hartwell, daughter of the veteran Dr. J. B. Hartwell (whose laundry was marked in Chinese characters "Chinaman's Friend") went to China in 1888. Miss Sallie Stein came back from China to Fresno, and four "lady teachers" were sent to China from this "nursery for foreign missionaries."

Devoted women volunteers joined the missionaries' work all up and down the coast; but their work, too, received opposition from the churches. In Chico some church members left when Chinese wanted to join. The pastor, though, preached from the text, "I will draw *all* men unto me," and the Chinese were admitted. An intransigent deacon fled to the Presbyterian church, only to find himself a fellow-member with some Digger Indians!

Some missionaries and Chinese pastors, such as Dong Gong in Portland, thought the Chinese should join American churches instead of forming their own. But as a rule, Mr. Hartwell said in 1887, the Chinese were not invited to attend and, if they attended on their own, were met with coldness or even rudeness.

The missionaries thought it was a wonder the Chinese would even dream of becoming Christians, considering how they were treated. The small proportion of women and their lack of freedom made it hard for them to serve the Chinese. But the teaching of English was a valuable service to children and mothers. In the 1880s and 1890s, schools and English classes for the Chinese were started by women in New York, Montana, Utah, Illinois, and the length of the Pacific Coast.

The Chinese mission school conducted on behalf of the Women's Baptist Home Mission Society in San Francisco became one of the finest. Mildred Cummings, western area missionary supervisor whose name is also associated with Indian missions, was first sent there. The work was carried on down through the years. In the 1940s and 1950s Celia Allen, missionary appointee to the First Chinese Baptist Church, did a notable service.

Things were changing by then in Chinatown. The pastors were still Chinese-speaking, but the young were growing up American in language and culture. They could not make themselves understood. Celia Allen took up for them. She helped them plan outings and activities, American style, and backed their proposal for a room of their own—"just a cubby-hole at first," Dorothy Bucklin recalls. The energy and ability of these young people surged irresistibly ahead. In 1953 three of them were ordained into the ministry: James Chuck, Edmund Fung, and John Tan. Edmund Fung served as pastor of the Community Baptist Church in San Mateo, then became a chaplain in the U.S. Army, where he now has the rank of major. Donald Jee was ordained later and became minister at Sacramento. Anna Louie, Maelene Jong, and others have always been involved in professional or lay Christian work.

These are now some of the most productive leaders in the American Baptist denomination. The First Chinese Baptist Church of San Francisco shows a kind of progress unusual in contemporary churches.

The pastor, Dr. James Chuck, said:

During the more than twenty years that I have been pastor of the church, the people who were baptized with me during the 1940's and early 1950's have grown up and now hold responsible positions within the church and in the community at large. Celia Allen, who was the last missionary under appointment at the church, provided the continuity from the missionary to the classic church period. When she began, the pastor's responsibility was focused primarily on the Sunday morning worship service; while the missionaries carried on much of the day by day programs and ministries of the church. Now, lay people assume responsibilities once largely assumed by missionaries. When lay people assume responsibilities for the work of the church, the church grows. The present active membership of the church is 360, with numerical growth continuing at a steady rate each year, even though the church is affected by high mobility of membership characteristic of urban areas.[4]

This church has weathered not only the early conflict between Chinese-oriented elders and English-speaking youths, but also the later strain which occurred when assimilated young people took power away from the elderly and seemed inhospitable to Chinese-speaking immigrants. The number of these increased greatly in 1965, after a change in immigration laws, causing the church to call Rev. James Yang, who originally came from Hong Kong but attended college and seminary in this country, to develop programs for these new immigrants.

Astrid Peterson speaks of the unity that has developed in the First Chinese Baptist Church since she came in 1953. "The English-speaking people used to meet in Fellowship Hall, the Chinese-speaking in the sanctuary. All officers of the church except a few old deacons were English-speaking."[5] Now they often meet together.

Astrid Peterson had been sent to China in 1930 from the Swedish Baptist Church in Kingsburg, California. When the missionaries had to leave China, she became a missionary to the Chinese in San Francisco. Now that she is retired, she belongs to the church and teaches in the English-language night school, which is again vital to the community. Sarah Downer, another former missionary to China, teaches there, too.

Massive Chinese immigration has not set the pendulum swinging back toward Chinese language domination in the church, but it has strengthened ethnic self-affirmation. Dr. Chuck is active in the National Conference of Chinese Churches (interdenominational) and has been its president.

When Eddie Tong went as pastor to the Fresno Chinese Church in 1939, he found the work Frances Potter had begun in 1884 being carried on by Amy Purcell. Miss Purcell had found in Fresno "just one little old building" and had set about making a mission. She visited, set up the usual programs, and then broadened them by adapting elements of the Girl Reserves. She also led the Boy Scouts herself. She knew and loved the Bible—"loved it tenderly"—but tried not to be narrow. Someone had told her, "Miss Purcell, you know it isn't your denomination; it's your relationship to the Lord!"[6]

In all she did she was assisted by a volunteer worker, Ruth Nelson, an accountant, who gave her free time—four evenings a week and Saturday and Sunday afternoons—for a lifetime of service. Both women comment on how glad they are to see the change in Chinese work in fifty years: "Then they were alone, now all are together."[7]

Women volunteers had a great part, all up and down the coast, in carrying on work in Santa Ana, Oakland, Sacramento, and Tulare. Their work counted, in the even crueler times to come.

The Chinese were not the only ill-treated guests in California. The Japanese had been induced to come, in turn, by offers of what seemed high wages, which were yet substandard for the United States, thus building hostility among displaced workers. When the Japanese realized their mistake and demanded more, the employers turned on them. Then in 1908 the Japanese Exclusion Act was passed.

The Japanese women were especially destitute, some of them "mail-order brides." Mrs. Koshi Okazaki, the wife of a Japanese pastor in Seattle, begged the Baptist women to send a missionary to their aid. None was available, so the Society asked Mrs. Okazaki herself to take leadership, and the Japanese Baptist Woman's Home was begun in 1905. Other Japanese work was started, from Sacramento to Terminal Island (near San Pedro), and succeeded well.

The next thirty-five years saw many achievements in Chinese-American and Japanese-American communities, but they were still tight defensive enclaves. Restrictive laws (immigration and land-use) and economic discrimination kept them "in their place." For forty years, every session of the California legislature attempted to pass at least one anti-Japanese law. Soon Asians were barred from land ownership, and then from citizenship. But worse was to come.

Bernice Cofer says, "Where was I on December 7, 1941? I was teaching high school on the Columbia River east of Portland, an area where many Japanese-American truck farms and flower-growing families brought goods individually to the markets. The removal of all Japanese (alien or citizen) from the Pacific Coastal area affected some who had been my students."[8]

Bernice watched the brutal evacuation with horror. Hurried from their homes, forced to carry all their essential belongings on their own backs, they followed a new Trail of Tears to assembly centers and, after immense confusion, to concentration camps.

> Snow upon the rooftop,
> Snow upon the coal;
> Winter in Wyoming—
> Winter in my soul.[9]

This poem was written at the Heart Mountain Relocation Camp by a young girl, Miyuki Aoyama, well known later in Baptist circles as the secretary of Fred W. Anderson, of the San Francisco Bay Cities Union. It was published in the camp newspaper by the editor, Bill Hosokawa, and included in his book, *Nisei: The Quiet Americans.*

But what lay beyond what Miyuki spoke of as the "absolutely desolate, devastating" concentration camps? This question tortured Bernice Cofer until she got in touch with her friend Isabelle Gates, then Christian Friendliness missionary in Oregon. Bernice was relieved to find that her own denomination was working hard to alleviate what they could in the disaster. Bernice decided to give up teaching and join them. She was appointed as Christian Friendliness missionary in Northern California, where she remained for ten years. She says:

> We were actually able to go in and pick up the tune. . . . I got to Tule Lake (a center where many of the Issei, or foreign-born, evacuees—only a third of the total—were gathered) when the young Nisei (U.S.-born) were refusing to be repatriated to Japan with their parents. Thomasine Allen (long-time missionary in Japan) was helping—part of the matrix of Christian perspective that can absorb even the stress and strain of war and produce creative alternatives. . . .[10]

Bernice was one of those who met the first brave individuals to return to the San Francisco area when they were released. She helped them find shelter and tried to establish the extent of their financial loss (they were later repaid at about 10 cents to the dollar) in order to help them get started again. One great service of the Christian Friendliness Department was arranging the enrollment of students in midwestern and eastern universities that were willing to accept them.

The Christian Friendliness missionaries had the additional task of entertaining, with Baptist churches, Japanese educators who were sent to this country for democratic indoctrination, as part of the reparations. Friendly informality helped relax the tension and suspicion of the visitors.

The story did not turn out altogether badly, thanks to the amazing balance and adaptability of the victims, and to a degree of goodwill and experience from some Americans—notably missionaries and volunteers and those to whom they had communicated some of their understanding. The walls of separation, so rudely broken down, at least stayed down enough for the creativity as well as the integrity, industry, and thrift of the Japanese-Americans to pour into communities all over the country. Our own most cherished example is Jitsuo Morikawa.

Dorothy Stevens, formerly of the Board of Education and Publication, tells how a seminary group asked what they could send to this young Baptist pastor from the Los Angeles area, to help him pass the long time of dismal leisure. He asked for Kenneth Latourette's *History of Christianity.* He was preparing for an incalculably important contribution to the denomination and, indeed, the Christian world. He began his contribution as the first Japanese-American pastor of an integrated church; he then headed the Department of Evangelism, and later became associate executive secretary of the Board of National Ministries. Jitsuo Morikawa has stirred the denomination to its depths and raised it to new heights.

True to their genius, which includes love of the past as well as masterly adaptation to the present, the Japanese-American Citizens' League took action at the earliest opportunity to secure legislation to allow their parents to become citizens. The dedication of Bill Hosokawa's book expresses their feelings, and ours, concerning all the Asians who have made their homes in this country against such incredible odds.

*"To the Issei, who made it all possible."*

# 6

# The Cross Is Bending
## to the Earth

Anna Barkely, one of the first missionaries sent to Cuba by the women, was spending the night in a room with several other delegates to a convention.

One of the women wakened early and asked, "What time is it?"

Another glanced through the window and saw the Southern Cross sparkling against the dawn. "It is almost morning, for the cross is bending to the earth."

This is an illustration of how the women missionaries felt when the power of Spain over Mexico and Central America was broken. Now at last the true gospel could be brought to Latin America! In 1869 when Benito Juarez won reform and religious freedom for Mexico, Baptists immediately began to consolidate the small brave work begun before 1830 by a Scottish Baptist colporteur. A missionary was appointed in 1870, but he remained only briefly. Fortunately "a few heroic Christian women" who had banded together in 1874 as the Mexican Baptist Mission Society continued the work for several years.

American women were much interested in the mission school opened by the ABHMS in Monterey in 1882. Soon they began appointing teachers and opening schools on their own. Mexican young women were trained at Baptist Missionary Training School (BMTS) and went back to their country to work, along with American graduates. Some Mexican women were appointed without training.

> Concepcion Renteria, a venerable sister, whose services were highly prized, and whose praise was in all our Mexican churches, was chosen to fill the vacancy occasioned by the marriage of Epifania Trevino in October, 1887.[1]

Work was interrupted by the Revolution, but reestablished as soon as possible. In 1910, the Colegio Bautista Howard in Puebla, Mexico, became a fully graded school with a normal and missionary training department and was a significant force among the more liberal Catholics. It was here that Rena Button did much of her work, beginning in 1928.

Rena, like the Rishels, Mary Lake, Mabel Young, and many others, worked wherever she could. Women in Mexico were always reminded that they were the helpers and were not expected to make major decisions in the churches. But they were welcome to labor in the Sunday school, help with young people's organizations, and do women's work. Rena expanded on these possibilities. She organized a children's church in Puebla, which produced many young pastors and lay workers. She translated seven quarters of the Judson Keystone Series Junior Department lessons, publishing it with no help but that of a part-time secretary. She brought out a bimonthly "Bulletin of Christian Education" on the mimeograph. In 1955 she published a book called *Materiales Visuales en la Educacion Cristiana,* the first visual aid published in Spanish, which was used by the public schools in 1956 and 1957. She cooperated with the department of Christian Education of the Council of Churches in the organization of CAVE (Centro Audio Visual Evangelico) and was elected its first president. This center is still active in providing audiovisual materials in Mexico. She taught Christian Education at the Baptist Seminary in Mexico City from 1950–1961. One of her students is now the director of CAVE.

Another outstanding woman in Mexico developed her work beyond expectations. Dr. Ota G. Walters, who as she worked in the Puebla Hospital Latino Americano became aware of the desperate unmet need of Indians in the Oaxaca mountains, packed up and went out to find them. She was the only foreigner and the only evangelical in Miahuatlán, and at first she met hostility. But her service soon won acceptance, and she was joined by a young pastor.

When the Spanish-American War released Cuba and Puerto Rico from the control of Spain in 1899, the missionaries thronged to the Islands. Miss Elma G. Gowan in Cuba and Mrs. Janie P. Duggan in Puerto Rico were the first workers sent by the Woman's Home Mission Society. The missionaries had just arrived in Puerto Rico when the island was visited by a hurricane, which caused thousands of deaths. The climate was hard on the newcomers, and travel conditions were excruciating. One letter speaks of a mission trip during which, from Tuesday until late Sunday, the missionary never took off his clothing, but slept on canvas cots and hammocks, wooden benches, and chairs, climbed slippery mountain trails on foot and horseback, crossed rushing rivers swollen by rain, went where Americans had never been before, and came back feeling "that the Lord had many saints in these hills."

Under such circumstances, some of the exhilaration must have ebbed, and many of the eager recruits had to return home with broken health. But the women kept on.

*"Santiaguito!"* called Ester Palacios, and the little boy came running. He liked the little dark Indian woman from Nicaragua (who had gone to Brooklyn as a maid, become converted, and been called to the mission field), and he liked her tall, blonde sidekick from Oklahoma, Adell Martin. He liked what they taught him at the Center at Caguas.

A few years later, little Santiago suffered an injury and nearly died. When he recovered, his mother in gratitude dedicated him to the church. He was a useful gift.

Santiago Soto-Fontanez attended the University of Puerto Rico, the Puerto Rico Seminary, and Biblical Seminary in New York. He received his Ph.D. from Columbia University. He served as pastor in Puerto Rico and Brooklyn, taught many years at Brooklyn College, headed the Spanish-speaking work of the New York Baptist City Societies, and became the first executive of the Association of Spanish-Speaking Baptist Churches of Metropolitan New York.

Dr. Soto was instrumental in the formation of the Spanish Caucus, became its second president, and still serves as consultant. He is also translating curriculum into Spanish for the Board of Educational Ministries. The Santiaguito of Ester and Adell is one of the key figures in Hispanic Baptist work in the U.S. His mother, alert and well at 107, rejoices in his achievements.

Responsibility for Puerto Rican work was early shared by the people of the Island. The Aaron Webbers, arriving in 1931, found that already there were few outsiders, and no North American occupied a pastorate. From about 1945 there was a fine reciprocal relationship between the Puerto Rico Baptist Convention and the ABHMS and the WABHMS. Laura Fish and, later, Ruth Maldonado were made members of the Convention Board as representatives of the two Societies.

Ruth Maldonado received her nurse's training in Puerto Rico, and then she went to BMTS. She became Puerto Rico's Director of Christian Education under Dr. Oscar Rodriguez and has carried on that work since, in what Dorothy Bucklin calls an unassuming but wonderfully effective way.

The Webbers felt on their recent return for the seventy-fifth anniversary of Puerto Rican work that this former mission field had itself become mission.

Puerto Rico, with the status of a state convention, self-determining, and represented on the ABC board and agencies, serves as a bridge, as Dr. Charles S. Detweiler called it long ago, between the United States and other Latin American countries.

The distinguished brothers Adam and Benjamin Morales, who have contributed so much to Mexican and Mexican-American life, were brought into Aiken Christian Center in Chicago. This was the beginning of a lively friendship between them and Mrs. Millard Collins, then Helen Schmitz, Eastern Area mission counselor and secretary for communications of the WABHMS. Thus the Latin-American work of the women makes contributions to the work in the United States while the U.S. work supplies resources to Latin America.

In 1916, the Congress on Christian Work in Latin America requested the Baptist missionary societies to send missionaries to the three central republics of Central America: Nicaragua, El Salvador, and Honduras.

There was a woman already on the field. She was Eleanor Blackmore, who had arrived in Costa Rica in 1902 from a Baptist deaconess home in Chester. She had been driven by her sympathies to bring nursing help to yellow fever sufferers. But she had no sooner arrived than she herself contracted the fever. The doctor refused to treat her, saying, "No hope, she will die before morning." As she heard the retreating hoofbeats of the doctor's horse, she thought, "Well, if I am to die in the morning, I shall die game." She didn't die game, not that day, anyway, but she certainly lived game. She went on to Nicaragua where she founded the "School of the Living Christ," supported by a faith mission. When the faith of the mission burned high, she received funds; but when faith dimmed, she was reduced to living on starch. Nevertheless, she persisted. When the Baptists were given the chance to work in Nicaragua, Miss Blackmore was adopted by the women.

But her troubles were not over. The Roman Catholics, long entrenched in Nicaragua and unused to challenge, were affronted by the evangelical intrusion and tried to destroy it.

When the meetinghouse was attacked, Miss Blackmore locked up and gathered her forces in solid ranks to face down the intruders. But her best defense, and that of the other missionaries in similar circumstances, was the loving concern and habitual helpfulness of Baptists toward all the people, particularly the neediest.

In 1918, some of the U.S. mission officials came to visit, among them Mrs. Katherine Storey Westfall, executive of the WABHMS for twenty-eight years. The VIP's were visiting in Diriamba when the word came, "Don't go back to Managua on the train tomorrow—it is to be attacked." Mrs. Westfall was a dauntless woman (she had been active in civil reform in Chicago, as well as in women's mission work) and would not be intimidated. But the party must have set out with mixed emotions.

Suddenly, as they passed through the rich coffee plantations, the train seemed to hesitate momentarily.

*"Hay cuatro malvados!"* someone yelled.

The engine accelerated. The four evildoers were startled, dropped their guns, and ran. The crucial moment came when the engineer refused to stop when challenged, having been forewarned of the planned attack by Ramon Perez, the station agent, a Baptist convert. "After that visit, the work grew steadily," an article in *Missions* for May, 1930, stated.[2]

Eleanor Blackmore's little school developed into a fine modern institution with a boarding department, achieving in 1962 equal standing with the National Institute, college level. An excellent boys' school had been built and was also in great demand.

During the middle of the century Mary Butler, itinerant missionary like Joanna P. Moore, went on trips throughout Nicaragua, stopping at churches, homes, and even along the roadside to tell stories and sing with the children. What did she take along on these trips? In a letter she recorded:

> My bed and bedding or a hammock if I know there will be no place for me to put up my cot, in which case I sling my hammock in the church; boiled water; my sun helmet; my personal clothing; phonograph and records; flannelgraph board and its materials; and of course all the books and materials I will need in teaching on a two weeks' trip. I should buy a stove and then I could go out for longer trips, but I can eat native food for only two weeks at a time.[3]

For some years, because of poor health she remained in the U.S. Later, when she found she was terminally ill, Mary Butler got permission from the WABHMS Board to go back to Nicaragua. She continued to hold institutes for pastors, sometimes from a chaise longue. She had her wish fulfilled, living out her life with the people she loved.

In 1927, the Evelyn Briggs Cranska Memorial Hospital was built in Managua. This fulfilled a poignant dream of the poor people of Nicaragua, who had added their pesos to the larger gifts. Earthquakes shook the buildings disastrously in 1931 and 1972, but buildings can be rebuilt, and the quality of personnel, from Dr. John S. Pixley, the first doctor in charge, to Ruth Curtis, the first nurse, has sustained its service and its reputation. Phoebe Rice (who became Mrs. Pixley) founded a Nurses' Training School famous throughout Central America.

The work in Honduras never developed, and neither did the unification of the three little countries, hoped for by the missionaries. But in El Salvador, a vigorous work has gone forward. Some of the most interesting projects have been invented and carried out by women appointed to work in El Salvador by the women's societies. Early women pioneered in the hinterlands as "muleback ministers," calling persons to Christ, healing them, and setting up vacation schools for them. Two women who served in schools founded by the WABHMS in El Salvador for thirty-five years and more were Ruth Carr and Evalena McCutcheon. These schools, in Santa Ana and San Salvador, achieved scholastic excellence and universal respect, preparing leaders who now function in the universities, in government, in business, and in the ministry.

Grace Hatler could not endure the poverty of the people amidst plenty; so she set up projects in nutrition, farming, and animal husbandry in the school at Santa Ana. She also initiated the founding of a home for the care of the aged. Volunteers, such as Rev. A. A. Cober, Mrs. Agnes Beckwith, and Florence Stansbury, a director of Christian education in the United States, came to enrich the program.[4]

When American Baptists sent a missionary to Haiti in 1923, a benign explosion occurred. (This was not the first Baptist work attempted there; a relative of the Orrin Judd family had served briefly just a hundred years earlier.) The deprived but eager people seized the idea of lay ministry; and a loaves-and-fishes miracle occurred. Soon one preacher was administering ten, twenty, and even more outstations which were led by lay leadership.

Mildred Benson, sent out as a teacher in 1958, found no women's work. Why? "Well, there are no leaders," was the answer. Women in Haiti had poor status, could not read, and had to work all the time anyway. Mildred was not daunted, and she began Dorcas Societies. When an embargo on used clothing was imposed by Haiti, the Dorcas Societies filled an important function. Their usefulness has strengthened their purpose and increased their scope. They participated in Bible study, prayer, projects of sewing for the poor, and visitation. One of their joys is the sponsorship of weddings. They actually make marriage seem possible to poor couples who have no decent clothes for the ceremony.

The reader of history is awed by the notable record of the women missionaries of Latin America, loving and giving without stint, suffering without complaint, and braving stiff ordeals. There was no easy air transport in those days. Sea journeys were long, and rail travel was in open-air trains crowded with chickens, ducks, and produce as well as human passengers. Missionaries' terms were seven years, menaced by tropical disease under inadequate medical care and threats of overt hostility from a noncomprehending culture. Such rigors are not imposed today nor are sacrifices from outsiders even accepted.

For example, in Mexico no institutional work remains in active relationship with American Baptists. That is not to say that all the love and work went for nought. Fraternal relationship remains, and help is still given, such as is illustrated by a letter from the Horeb Baptist Church of Mexico City. The pastor, Rolando Gutierrez-Cortes, writes that with the loan from American Baptist Extension Corporation (ABEC) the congregation was able to build its sanctuary which, besides serving its own church needs, entertains Bach concerts, youth services, continental congresses, the preaching of Nicky Cruz, ALFALIT (literacy) programs, prayers for the sick, and ministry to former drug addicts.

Roberto Porras, a Mexican pastor, says:

> The institutions established by ABHMS/WABHMS may not be there, but institutions are secondary. You began the work more than a century ago. Our leaders were trained by you. Many of the churches were built by loans from American Baptists. Education was provided. The philosophy of Mission was taught, which we follow today.[5]

Cubans surely remember, under the stress and challenge of their new life, the "Offering of the Talents." This was the idea, conceived by Elisa Infante in 1942, of distributing small sums to the presidents of the nineteen Woman's Societies and asking them to "multiply it for the Lord." It was much like the Love Gift in the American Baptist Churches in the U.S.A. and elicited the same devotion. The talents are surely being multiplied still in Cuba, though perhaps in different ways.

Still, it is hard not to be wistful over the loss of that excitement, that initiative. And it is more needed than ever.

The decade of the sixties, which was supposed to bring great progress in Latin America, is now seen to have been the worst in the history of the continent. Edward Kennedy said in 1970: "The Alliance for Progress has been a human failure. More than 30 percent of the population still die before their 40th birthday. Poverty, malnutrition and disease continue to deny strength and incentive to the majority of the people."[6]

How can this be, when the sixties began with the most imaginative program of inter-American cooperation ever conceived? This program planned massive agrarian reform, opportunity for political participation for all, taxation and education reforms, and an end to inherited privilege and class division.

Instead, a new style of imperialism has developed, with the U.S. and other industrialized countries entrusting power and money to small national elite groups who maintain order by force to protect international enterprise; and most of the profits go out of the country. Our benevolence has become a mockery, just as the goodwill of the Monroe Doctrine was belied by the Mexican War, and by no less than seventy U.S. military interventions between 1848 and the Santo Domingo incident in 1971. The economic help given through the Alliance for Progress resulted in a far greater flow of wealth from the poor nations to the rich than the other way around, causing the increasing and accelerating poverty noted above.

Where revolution attempts to reverse this destructive cycle, as in Cuba, the United States is alarmed and defensive. When repressive governments overpower democratic ones, as in Brazil and Chile, our interests seem bolstered, and we mistake this for improvement.

Yet Rafael Cepeda, internationally known ecumenical leader of Cuba, noted author and theologian, calls revolution "a judgment of God on the past, and at the same time, a new opportunity that God gives to love and serve as Jesus Christ did."[7]

For the most part, the churches that grew from missionary activity have come to serve a privileged middle sector, alienated from the struggle for liberation, so that the present role even of the evangelical church is in some ways very much like that of Roman Catholicism during the Spanish conquest.

However, there are notable exceptions. A few present-day missionaries dare government hostility as Eleanor Blackmore braved the attacks of the established church. Some are militant, engaging in guerrilla warfare in defense of the poor. Some are simply faithful, like Father Hector Gallego, who worked side by side with the oppressed peasants of Panama and disappeared in the dark of the night in June, 1971.[8]

About the same time that Hector Gallego disappeared, apparently kidnapped and probably killed by the government, a Baptist minister and seminary professor, Luis Rivera, finished a three-month prison term in Puerto Rico. He had participated with Quakers and others in building a religious chapel on a public beach. It was on the island of Culebra, where the U.S. Navy wanted to continue trying out its death weapons.

The cross is still bending to the earth.

# Part Two
# The Tree in the Sky

---

*"The Lord has seen to it that no tree grows up into the sky."**
German proverb

* Bertha Grimmell Judd, *Fifty Golden Years* (New York: The Du Bois Press, 1927), p. 152.

# 7

# The Roots

<blockquote>

We are the highway and hedge workers, who are also able to expound the Scriptures. We can help a tired mother cut out a garment for her child, and meanwhile teach both mother and child the Gospel. We not only pray for the sick, but we also cook them a tempting morsel of food. We are equally at home in parlor or kitchen. "Our shoes are iron and brass," there is no road too hard for us to travel.[1]

</blockquote>

Joanna P. Moore said this in her book, *In Christ's Stead,* but also in her life. It's a pretty good job description for the missionaries sent out from 1877 onward by the Women's Baptist Home Mission Society and the Woman's American Baptist Home Mission Society, the twin organizations based in Chicago and Boston, which later merged, taking the name of the eastern group, Woman's American Baptist Home Mission Society, but with headquarters in Chicago.

The women of the denomination had long been eagerly interested in the work of the Home Mission Society. Between 1845 and 1853, forty-three Female Mite Societies gave $12,438.91 to Home Mission projects. They were especially alert to the need for teachers and nurses for women and children. Yet the ABHMS Board, composed of men, hesitated to send out single women into the rigors of the mission field. The wives of men appointed to Indian fields or to the far Territorial frontiers went along and usually assumed a large share of the burdens, but they were not officially appointed. Appointing women to the mission field wasn't feasible. It wasn't proper. It wasn't biblical.

But Joanna P. Moore and others already in the field kept calling "until their eyes were dim and their voices faint"; they were impossible to ignore.

The Women's Home Mission Society of Michigan was formed in 1873 "for the evangelization of the freed people and other needy people in this country,"[2] and about the same time the Free Baptist Women organized for the same purpose. In February, 1877, the Women's Baptist Home Mission Society of Chicago proclaimed itself

> . . . a distinct department of home mission work never before undertaken by the denomination, and appealing especially to women, viz: A work by women in homes for the elevation and christianization of the families of the more degraded populations of our country—a work which, if secondary to the preaching of the Gospel, is almost vital to its complete success. . . .[3]

In November of the same year, the Woman's American Baptist Home Mission Society was organized at Tremont Temple, Boston, for

> the evangelization of the women among the Freed people, the Indians, the heathen immigrants, and the new settlements of the West.[4]

These two organizations absorbed smaller ones and launched into ambitious programs. They operated similarly, appointing missionaries and administering programs and raising money to meet their own budgets. In addition they told their story vividly, through articles in all Baptist magazines, and through *Tidings,* their own organ. They also told it as they appeared in churches throughout their areas. The Chicago society was known to be especially oriented to evangelism and the Boston society was oriented to education, but each undertook a full and rounded ministry.

The women must have startled the men by their boldness. The General Society (a term used by Charles White to distinguish ABHMS from the women's societies) made an abortive effort to control them. But the WABHMS replied:

> . . . as women can best judge the qualifications needed for woman's work, and as this Board is alone responsible for the financial prosecution of its work, whether in the establishment of auxiliaries, the collecting of funds, or support of its missionaries, it is fitting and necessary that it appoint its own missionaries and have command of its own treasury.[5]

By 1881, the Chicago women had appointed twenty missionaries, and a new problem had come up, or rather, a vast conglomeration of problems. Picture twenty young women of differing backgrounds and limited experience setting forth to evangelize and also Americanize a heterogeneous multitude of destitute freed people, dispossessed and traumatized Indians, homesick Europeans, Asians, and Caribbean and Mexican people!

"The work is too holy and too responsible to be committed to novices,"[6] the Chicago women stated (moderately). So they submitted a plan for a training school. Actually, they demanded the plan's adoption. They were backed by the force of four hundred auxiliary sections organized by the small but powerful Mary Burdette, the first employed executive of the WBHMS—the "Little General." This title described her courage and her administrative ability, but there was no condescension nor tyranny in her. She had "a merry heart which doeth good like a medicine." As corresponding secretary of the WBHMS, and later preceptress of the training school, she was leaven as well as loaf.

The plan was for a three- to six-month course with biblical, medical, and domestic instruction. The women were also required to participate in the kind of work they would be doing on the mission field. This was to test their adaptation to and love for service.[7]

Those women accomplished their goal starting in September, 1881, the first school in the world solely for the missionary training of women. It was called the Baptist Missionary Training School and was located in Chicago. In a few months they had rented a building, recruited sixteen students, several already workers in the field, and secured volunteer instructors of the caliber of Dr. Edgar J. Goodspeed, biblical translator. Other professors from the University of Chicago and pastors of Chicago churches also volunteered to teach. Mary Burdette's brother John taught a course in parliamentary law, and two women from the Columbia School of Oratory taught "speech delivery."

The Baptist Missionary Training School served well. The length of the course grew from three months to ten months to three years, and finally to four years. The size of the school grew from sixteen students to over one hundred, overflowing one building after another. At the May meetings of the WBHMS in 1904, Mrs. J. N. Crouse, who was then president of WBHMS, requested permission never before granted one agency—to solicit funds for a new building. As she stood, her notes cascaded to the floor. She made it an opportunity.

"I don't need notes to talk about Baptist Missionary Training School," she said. "What I want to say is fundamental. The work of the Women's Baptist Home Mission Society must not be handicapped by a mere lack of space for the applicants who are willing to enter service for their Christ."

Meanwhile, the sustaining substructure of the Training School and the Mission Societies was growing, as the "Little General" and others kept organizing, informing, and training the constituency. For many years, *Tidings,* edited by Mary Burdette, circulated news of field and school. It makes interesting reading today.

(1893) Miss Fannie Allen, our General Missionary for East Washington and North Idaho, sends a report of the convention held at Moscow . . . at the women's session she wishes to record the fact that the brothers did not, as is so often the case when a woman's meeting is announced, leave the room to attend to important committee work, but remained in a body throughout the session.

In 1897—

An hour was given our Women's Society in the evening of May 19 in which to present its work. This was the first public recognition of our Women's Society on the program of one of the national meetings of the denomination.

In 1902, the society voted to continue as a separate organization.

the work can be better administered by continuing the present auxiliary relations.

And in 1903, evidently in response to another overture by the General Board, the women voted "that we, as a Board, desire to continue as a separate organization, auxiliary to the ABHMS."

The support given BMTS was minimal. They had to work on a shoestring. It was a miracle they could get by, but they always expected miracles. They remained at a lamentably low wage scale, but with high energy.

Jennie Peck was a graduate of the first BMTS class. She had been crippled as a child and was unable to walk for twelve years. Finally she was able to get about on crutches, and she began to start Sunday schools in what she called "destitute country neighborhoods" of Iowa and Illinois. Then she became church and city missionary in Oskaloosa. Later she worked two years with Joanna P. Moore in New Orleans. By now it was 1881, and Jennie Peck enrolled in the first class at BMTS as both teacher and student. She said she helped cook the first meal, made the beds, and taught the first class. She became preceptress at the Caroline Bishop Training School in Dallas, taught at Leland University for twenty-three years, and in 1910 went to Washington as assistant superintendent for the National Training School for Negro Women. She retired in 1914 but continued to serve Negroes, Japanese, and Chinese in Washington. In 1929 she went to live in California and did volunteer work among the Mexicans until she could no longer get around.

Marguerite Stifler, who graduated from BMTS in 1883, went to Tucson to work among the Mexicans. This was the raw frontier. She wrote of General Crook's victory, "The hostiles are finally conquered, and Arizona feels that henceforth she will be safe!" She worried about the Mexicans: ". . . these wretched hovels! . . . babies suffer here. They have no floors and the alkali in the soil makes the tender flesh very sore." She prayed for a worker who could help the people with their kitchen gardens, and she longed to master the language. She found the American citizens of Tucson "a lofty, almost unapproachable class of infidels, who think that religion may be a good thing for ignorant Mexicans who cannot think for themselves." She also liked teaching the Chinese who had come into that area. She inquired, "Why are you a sinner?" "Muchee bad think," was the reply.[8]

"I fear the dogs more than anything else," she wrote. ". . . I put a store box in front of one door and two chairs . . . in front of the other. . . . I am getting quite brave, and I think I will before long get used to frontier life, except the *wickedness,* which is *appalling.*"[9]

Martha J. Ames, an 1887 graduate, went through the San Francisco earthquake with the Chinese and was quarantined with them for the bubonic plague. She felt this quarantine was harassment, pure and simple, because none of the Chinese had had the plague. She conducted school and meetings in her home; this opened the way for the First Chinese Baptist Church of San Francisco.

Eva Button graduated in 1891 and went to work with Joanna P. Moore. Then she went to the Indians of South Dakota. She became pastor-at-large in South Dakota in the twenties. The state secretary said, "When a church is in such bad condition that no man would undertake to save it, I send Miss Button."[10]

The audacious "I'll-tackle-anything" spirit did not go out with the pioneer days. Another graduate, Marie Seafler Ball, who graduated in 1942, was sent into a burgeoning war industry community in Omaha, Nebraska, to start a small church. She succeeded so well that after the war Dr. Herschel Caldwell, state secretary in Washington, called her to a Church Extension post in Washington. Before she was through, she had started ten churches! How did she do it?

"You find a place and you start to work!" Sometimes she made false starts. One time she arranged to live and hold her services in an abandoned restaurant which was strategically located in a flow of traffic. She found there was no heat and no water heater. She called the whole deal off. "Selfish? *God* called it off!" And sure enough, she found a better place, and by Easter she had seventy members. Another time she bought a Catholic church building and used it to found a Baptist church. Marie would stay in a place about a year. By then it would be well organized and ready—for a man.

Sometimes it was hard to leave, hard to keep her talents within the boundaries others made for her. At Kenewich, Washington, when they said she could only have a Sunday school, no church, she said, "No. They're going to have to listen to me. It's just God using me."

After all, women had been used by God before. There was Miriam. Endless missionary women had testified out of conviction and out of necessity. Dorothy Bucklin writes of Emma Sparswick and Mary Jayne and Hattie Everts, who in 1896 alternated with the minister in conducting preaching services to the Cheyenne-Arapahoes in Kingfisher and Watonga, Oklahoma. How many have done it with no comment and no recognition?

Dr. Caldwell valued Marie's work, and also her, as a person. They were married in 1958.

Elizabeth Allport, a 1920 graduate, spent thirty-five years in Cuba in various churches and in the school supported by the Guantanamo Baptist Church. She devoted herself to the establishment of World Wide Guild chapters.

The founding or inspiring of other training schools was another achievement of BMTS. Such schools were established in Dallas, Memphis, and Washington, D.C.; and Training Departments in Puebla, Mexico (1919), and Rio Piedras, Puerto Rico (1923), were spiritual daughters of BMTS.

BMTS encountered difficulties in the mid-twentieth century. It had worked under the wing of the WABHMS, sustained by small regular contributions from local women's societies, and it did not have the resources to meet the demands of technological education and the strain of inflation.

Though the curriculum had been well planned and had developed through the years, undergraduate training no longer prepared students adequately for the complex work they had to undertake. Preparation for professional work required special study at the graduate level, and students went where they could get such training.

In 1961 Pearl Rosser, president of BMTS, and Gene Bartlett, president of Colgate-Rochester Divinity School, concluded that the merger on which the two boards had decided would serve the needs of both schools. BMTS would receive the benefit of a splendid accredited graduate program at the seminary and would see its assets enable CRDS to take a large step forward in recognizing the place of women in the ministry. Cay Raycroft, president of the BMTS Alumnae Association, reflects on this event.

> When BMTS merged with CRDS, many of us who were alumnae were saddened by the loss of the visible image which for me stood at 510 Wellington Ave. It was a long time before I realized that for other alumnae, BMTS was represented by an image on Vernon Ave. or Indiana Ave. It has taken us over ten years to stop feeling sorry for what was, and to aggressively implement the BMTS purpose in American Baptist Churches today.

When Alice Brimson, president of BMTS from 1926 to 1937, resigned to become executive secretary of the WABHMS, Mrs. John Nuveen, past president of WABHMS, exclaimed, "Oh, Miss Brimson, to think you could give up all those lovely girls!"

Miss Brimson says she often wondered if she should have. The days of closeness with the girls and intimate knowledge of the work they were doing were most precious to her.

"I can still see the light flowing through their transoms!" she said. That light flowed far.

Meanwhile, the societies developed along their parallel lines. However, in 1909, after the American Baptist Convention came into being, they came together as a cooperating agency of the Convention. In 1919, like all the other agencies, they surrendered the privilege of raising their own funds.

In 1921, the Committee of Conference was organized, including representatives from the boards of both societies. The National Committee on Woman's Work, formed in 1937, was replaced in 1951 by the National Council of American Baptist Women. This ended, for the most part, the direct approach of the Mission Societies to the local church women. It put the job of understanding and undergirding mission into the hands of lay women.

# 8
## The Branches

"Come on, wash up now." This was the first item on the program. The children eagerly complied. It was a treat to use the clean running water and good toilet facilities provided by the canning company in the shed which had been loaned to the Home Missions Council for its summer children's program.

The program included a morning of play and learning, supervised free play in the afternoon for the children, and family club and social activities in the evening. In addition, workers found time to visit the old barracks from World War II in which each family occupied a ten-by-sixteen-foot room; they cooked, ate, and slept in it.

This was a better setup than many migrant workers had across the country through the twenties, thirties, forties, and indeed up to this very day. Some migrant laborers are housed in sheds, huts, chicken coops, and disused (but still odorous) sheep barns. The children have had to go along to the fields, school-age ones working because there were no schools they could fit into, toddlers tethered like puppies, and babies sheltered from the sun by propped-up blankets, because there was no one with whom to leave them. Some babies who were left home alone have burned in the sudden fires that strike inadequate housing.

Yet the people have maintained their humanity. When helped, they have responded, have taken giant steps, and have expressed appreciation.

> She gave me fifty cents,
> The little, speaking of the much within. . . .
> It glowed like gold.[1]

Thus wrote one of the more than two hundred summer workers in 1947, referring to a woman migrant she had helped. The worker was not a Baptist, but Baptists were working in such jobs, and Baptists had been in on the start of the Council of Women for Home Missions that had been truly responsible for this only substantial service to agricultural migrant laborers until the days of César Chávez.

Baptist women have always been interested in ecumenical efforts. It was a "stiff little Baptist," self-named, who helped crystallize into functional organizations the ecumenical spirit that had been stirring among women for half a century. When Helen Barrett (later to be Mrs. Montgomery) walked out on the Communion service at Wellesley because it was not properly "close," she didn't really want to, but felt that, as a loyal Baptist daughter, she had to.

However, her inner compulsion toward unity prevailed and helped to move the American Baptist women toward ecumenicity. Another Baptist, also born in 1861, worked right along with her to establish both Baptist and ecumenical Women's Foreign Mission organizations. Lucy Waterbury was widowed while working in India as a missionary's wife. At twenty-eight, she became assistant secretary of the Women's Baptist Foreign Mission Society. (Later she married again and became Lucy Peabody.)

Helen Schmitz Collins reminds us that the Home Mission Board has always been immensely in debt to the Foreign Mission Board, which got started six years earlier. The women's drive toward interdenominationalism in Home Missions was sparked by the early interdenominational foreign mission conferences in London in 1888, and in New York in 1900, where women for the first time helped make the plans. Lucy Waterbury was one of the five who organized the first Ecumenical Foreign Missions study, for which Helen Barrett Montgomery wrote one of the first books and produced more study books than any other author. Later, she was the first woman to translate the New Testament from Greek into English. She wanted to give the New Testament to ordinary people by removing "the veil" of literacy and formal language. These two women helped found the first summer school of missions and soon added home to foreign studies.

Another Baptist woman, Mrs. George W. Coleman, who had been for nineteen years president of the Boston WABHMS and then became the first president of the united WABHMS, was also first president of the interdenominational home mission societies, the Council of Women for Home Missions, founded after the Home Missions Council.

The Home Missions Movement had pushed westward across the country in sectarian singleness of purpose. The denominations pursued the pioneers in small, individualistic, almost anarchistic contingents, establishing hard-won beachheads, fighting the fighting individualism of the frontier.

The Baptists were a free and responsive agency for the kind of vital evangelism sparked by the Great Awakening and made to order for a new, crude, vigorous country beginning to feel the need for regeneration.

Notable Baptists, like John Mason Peck and Jonathan Going, prospected the new settlers and in 1832 helped organize the American Baptist Home Mission Society for a campaign they expected would continue for a century. But they could not foresee the complications or the need for joint action with other denominations.

Denominational rivalry for the lost lasted through the 1800s, but the difficulties of the task and the success of ecumenical foreign mission collaboration brought about the establishment of the National Federation of Churches, the Home Missions Council, and in 1906, the Interdenominational Committee for Women for Home Missions.

The development of the Home Missions Council and the Council of Women for Home Missions ran parallel for the first ten years of their development as unified agencies. Both were devoted to facilitating and unifying evangelistic efforts of their member denominations. Both believed education, public relations, and the establishment of comity and cooperation to be their functions.

But during the turbulent period of increasing immigration and world war, followed by rapid social disintegration, the idea of a more basic responsibility seized both organizations.

> Home Missions is the work of winning to Jesus Christ, and of training for Christian leadership, those who are disadvantaged by geographical, economic, industrial, racial, linguistic or historical conditions, and those who are handicapped by adverse circumstances from the development of full personality.[2]

Once noted, the predicaments of minorities burst through tidy generalities: the Japanese, viciously deprived of their basic civil rights in California; the awful unending injustice suffered by blacks; the tyrannical fluctuation in Indian policy; and the callous disinheritance of the migrants. Walter Rauschenbusch and Washington Gladden thundered with echoes of Isaiah and Amos upon the sensitive consciences of the middle-class Christians who comprised the Home Missions Councils.

The Council of Women, in its Annual Report for 1916, had said:

The attitude of the church has usually been turned away from the social to individual obligations. The privileges, rights and obligations of the individual have been paramount and only as modern inventions have forced capitalists into partnerships and trusts, and laborers into unions has the church awakened to new conditions and gone to the word of God for its helpful message, realizing that the Bible has a social message and meaning. There is an ever-widening gulf between the women of the church and the women in industry, working women are drifting away from the church and a feeling of antagonism is arising. The church must take an interest in these matters and must enter upon a propaganda of education for social justice and righteousness. The Christianizing of America in no small way depends upon getting in touch with industrial workers.

The Council of Women cooperated with the Joint Committee, made up of members of the Home Missions Council and the Council of Women for Home Missions, in efforts to bring social welfare to the masses, in Indian work, Negro work, Alaskan and Spanish-speaking work, Oriental and European immigrant work. But the new development of the twenties, and that in which women took the dominant and pioneering part, was work among migrant laborers. At the annual meeting of the two organizations in 1920, the work among women and children was allocated to the Women's Board. The women felt that it was time to go beyond mere focusing on and publicizing of a need, referring it for action to denominational boards. They felt they must sponsor direct missionary operations. By the summer of 1925, there were almost a dozen active programs among migrants across the country, administered by full-time directors, with the help of local groups and volunteers. The women's social awareness was intensified by this experience.

Though the two councils were cooperating more and more, fundamental differences began to emerge. As Robert Handy sums it up in his history of the Home Missions movement, *We Witness Together:*

Those who attended meetings of the Home Missions Council were mainly denominational secretaries with full-time mission responsibilities. Those who attended meetings of the Council of Women were predominantly members of the boards of the constituent societies and were often without full-time administrative responsibilities. In part because of this basic dissimilarity, the two Councils functioned somewhat differently. The Council of Women had a more detailed constitution and supervised its committees more closely. It was inclined to develop particular projects around which intense loyalties gathered—in this it followed the pattern of the denominational women's societies.[3]

Moreover, the Council of Women had a lot more money. They had developed their relationship with local interdenominational groups and a constellation of profitable services and publications. They also participated in stated events like the World Day of Prayer, and they collected dues from member societies.

In all areas of the women's work, the issues of the period were embodied. The trend toward uniting across denominational lines and the Social Gospel Movement were both vividly exemplified. And the women operated increasingly with independence along their own lines. They resisted merger every year. When on December 9, 1940, the Home Missions Council and the Council for Women finally merged, Dr. Mark Dawber and Miss Edith Lowry became joint secretaries. Men and women alternated as presidents of the board.

The influence of Baptists in the ecumenical movement continued, notably because of the activity of Anna Canada Swain on the Central Committee of the World Council of Churches. Others served on the National Board of the United Church Women. This ecumenical work no doubt enriched Baptist women's resources in many ways.

At the Northern Baptist Convention in Indianapolis in 1922, the issues of cooperative and social action, which had emerged and had been so strongly championed by women, were challenged by conservative members of the Baptist Convention. An effort was made to establish a statement of belief known as the New Hampshire Confession of Faith. This would, in effect, have made the noncreedal Baptists adopt a creed.

The effort was turned aside by the convention's agreement on a substitute motion by Dr. Cornelius Woelfkin: "The Northern Baptist Convention affirms that the New Testament is sufficient grounds for our faith and practice, and we need no other statement."

It was appropriate that the presiding officer at this meeting should have been Helen Barrett Montgomery.

# 9

# The Flowering

A small Jewish child had fallen seriously ill in the night. When the doctor came in the morning, he asked the mother why he hadn't been called sooner, since the symptoms had been alarming. She explained that she had no phone.

"But couldn't you have used a neighbor's phone?" he asked.

"You don't understand," she answered, "my neighbors are all Christians."[1]

This incident, related in *The World at My Door,* by Mary Martin Kinney, secretary of Christian Friendliness from 1926 to 1947, is a grim reflection on the failure of Christian America to work out humane relationships with the forty million newer immigrants who arrived between 1820 and 1920.

The church was not unaware of its duty to the strangers. The efforts of both General and Woman's Societies to retrieve the newcomers from their "degradation" were vigorous, resulting in foreign language churches in thirty different languages. The churches became strongholds, collecting small groups of nationals, forming their own associations, and gradually taking over their own support. They were useful as havens, but they remained largely hemmed in by ethnicity. And the English-speaking churches felt only secondary responsibility to the newcomers, not sharing the Roman Catholic idea that a church is answerable to God for all those who live within its parish.

However, the dynamics of Christianity make a perceived injustice intolerable, and projects grew up spontaneously. When BMTS included "Industrial" in its curriculum, field work among the foreign-speaking groups had already been started, and the young volunteers were welcomed as visitors and leaders in club programs that were known as Industrial Schools. These led, in the tens and twenties, to the development of the Christian Centers.

In 1912, the women launched a survey to find out who the immigrants were, why they had come to this country, and what help they were receiving. This survey resulted in 1913 in a study book by Mrs. Lemuel Call Barnes, dedicated "To the Strangers Within our Gates." This book revealed that public schools, labor unions, settlement houses, and other agencies, such as the YWCA and YMCA, did serve some needs. But the woman immigrant, locked in her home by tradition and language difference, was culturally abandoned by her husband and children as they exercised their larger options. In response to this discovery, Mrs. Barnes organized the Fireside League for the Teaching of English, and the same year Mrs. Alonzo M. Petty started a similar program in California.

When the United States became involved in World War I, the churches participated fully in that "common enterprise which [was] to release the spirit of the world from bondage." Then having helped make the world safe for democracy, Christian America realized it was about time to make democracy more safe in America; and in 1919 the Home Missions Council, in a study program, used Baptist Mission Secretary Charles A. Brook's *Christian Americanization,* the first study book to sell over 100,000 copies. It was a thoughtful as well as a timely book, redeeming any chauvinistic implications by its emphasis on the need to overcome prejudice and pride, to secure just economic and social conditions for everyone, and to appreciate the con- tributions as well as the needs of other national groups.

The same year, WABHMS organized its Christian Americaniza- tion Department. This entirely new sort of program was intended to go beyond the missionary work already serving the foreign-speaking groups within the institutional structure.

All women were to go about doing good, as Jesus had done. As Augustine put it, "one soul would set another on fire." Then a far- flung evangelization of foreign-born persons, such as a small staff of paid workers could never accomplish, would result, it was hoped.

Calling on the initiative of every woman was an inspiration, but the women knew they had to do more than that. They must work together, have accurate knowledge of what they were about, and train effective leaders.

A Christian Americanization Committee was set up in every district, state, and association. Their responsibility was to organize a community service in every church, to demonstrate the principles of Jesus Christ so graphically as to secure "real democracy in our own land, and peace and good will among men everywhere."

Miss Alice Brimson, primed and made ready by her own

outstanding work as volunteer World Wide Guild secretary for Illinois, speaker, and organizer, was called to head and train a professional staff, which would in turn organize and train the volunteers.

The person-to-person concept was broadened to include the church community. "Experiments in Christian Friendliness" called for month-long programs entered into by paired churches and included discussion, preaching, and other projects that might spring up spontaneously.

"Christian Americanization" seemed to some a patronizing and nationalistic title, and under the leadership of Mary Martin Kinney, the name was changed to "Christian Friendliness." Some objected to that name, too, as implying a more easy sentimental approach than what the need required. But it did express the women's hope of changing fear and hostility toward strangeness into understanding and friendship.

From 1948 to 1953, Isabelle Gates, now Mrs. Richard Rosenfels, headed the Christian Americanization Department. The world upheaval following World War II sent refugees fleeing in all directions, and the International Refugee Organization of the UN appealed to Church World Service, which solicited help from the Baptist World Alliance. Isabelle Gates and a pastor, Harold C. Bonnell, were sent to Europe to interview the refugees suffering and restless in camps. Some of these refugees could be relocated, if they fulfilled rigorous immigration requirements, by having someone in a host country assure jobs and residences.

"I was responsible for a staff which could be of enormous help in actually finding the sponsors," Isabelle Gates Rosenfels writes, "a staff which had the experience and know-how and contact with ABC churches to get the job done."

Four hundred dossiers were sent out, and hosts were found for almost all of them. But only 180 cleared the 25-part immigration hurdles. These "displaced persons" came from all parts of the world. The adoptive church communities continued their neighborliness during the first hard months of adjustment. They struggled with some hard problems but enjoyed insights and delights (symbolized for one church member by memory of the delicate grace of Indonesian candle-dances) and important, sustained relationships.

In the meantime a new opportunity arose, or an old one, long neglected, forced recognition by its urgency. The tractor revolution (the use of machines to do harvesting) had uprooted millions of black and white rural Southerners and sent them fleeing Northward, the blacks to the hellish refuge of ghettoized slums. An interim Christian Friendliness secretary, a self-styled "mere volunteer," focused the conscience of Christian Friendliness on this situation.

Mabel Martin, twin sister to a long-term missionary nurse, Helen Benjamin, had planned to go with her sister as a missionary doctor, but George Martin came along. He diverted her from the particular plan, but not from the life-style. Mabel tells a story which brings her husband into our narrative: Visiting in Japan, Mabel was told about the trouble Japanese women were having escaping from their limited role of impeccable wife, mother, and housekeeper. Therefore, Mabel fascinated both young and old by recounting how her husband told her he was marrying not only a woman, wife, and he hoped mother, but also a responsible person who carried out civic and religious duties to the full of her capacity. Mabel fulfilled his hopes.

She was admirably qualified for interim secretary, through experience as a member of the Board of Managers of WABHMS, as chairman of the Committee of Christian Friendliness, and through service in Church Women United as national chairman and vice-president. She made two notable contributions beyond her stated duties.

She encouraged the board to raise the professional status and salary scale of the Christian Friendliness staff. She would not tolerate the idea that people who had "heard the call" should be undervalued with meager salaries. She upgraded her department, starting a trend throughout the organization.

And Mabel was the one, Bernice Cofer, Christian Friendliness Secretary from 1954-1960, tells us, who forcefully put the question: "Who *is* our neighbor?"

When that "stimulus to moral regeneration," *Linda Brown* v. *Board of Education,* came in 1954, the women were ready. The Christian Friendliness Department promptly brought out a book, *Racial Integration in the Church,* an anthology of pieces by Christian Friendliness and other denominational staff, asserting that integration and mutual friendship were essential elements in all educational and evangelistic programs of the ABC. Much of this material was already extant, and the ease with which more could be assembled reflected the fact that the moral regeneration of the Baptists was already begun. All the women needed was a way of expressing their readiness to do the decent thing. And a means was found. This new approach was based on a book, *Know Your Neighbors,* by Rachel DuBois and Mew-soong Li.

Gordon W. Allport, Harvard Professor of Psychology, wrote in the Foreword: "One session employing the group conversation technique . . . seems to me to teach more about the common ground of ethnic and religious groups than many hours of lectures."[2]

Christian Friendliness introduced it, and the American Baptist Women took it up with enthusiasm, sending deputations to train leaders, enlisting states and associations. A typical session would start with the question, "I wonder if we can remember where we were when we were ten years old?" All would start to think back, getting *in under* present doubts and fears. "Did we do any work at that age?" All around the circle, people would light up with memory, and hesitantly, then eagerly, they would share their treasures: "What kind of bread did our mothers bake and serve? . . . What holidays did we celebrate? Remember the songs we used to sing?—Let's sing them!" Songs, dances, laughter, and tears. People recognized each other. Groups *became.*

"Ninety percent spontaneity, ten percent structure," Rachel DuBois says.

The old experiments in Christian Friendliness were updated, geared to a new psychological understanding, in what Margaret Mead called "a very important social invention."

When the Civil Rights movement got under way, past participants in group conversations met again at the barricades, in Washington, Selma, and Birmingham. And in 1965, Martin Luther King recruited Rachel DuBois to train black and white leaders in twelve Southern cities to support demonstrations and heal ruptures.

Women began to recognize the need and opportunity also for greater international understanding. Mabel Martin, a dedicated volunteer, represented the WABHMS on the Council for Christian Social Progress. In 1950, Don Cloward, head of the Council for Christian Social Progress, in a move characteristic of his discernment and innovativeness, asked Mabel to act for him as the official American Baptist nongovernmental representative at the United Nations. In this role Mabel attended briefing and questions sessions of the U. S. Mission to the United Nations and reported in articles and speeches to the churches. She contributed more than twenty-five years to this service which has now been extended by the addition of a field representative for the Division of Social Ministries, Eleanore Schnurr, who is enlarging Baptist influence by her knowledgeable and deft cultivation of relationships.

But the UN is not very effective, some people say.

"What else have we?" Mabel answers. If we keep in touch with and learn more about what is happening all over the world, and particularly in the countries in which our mission is established, we can gain what Mabel calls *trans-national* consciousness and see things not only in short-run terms and close-up, but also more nearly in the light of justice for all in this global village we call earth.

Another accomplishment of innumerable women working together has been the White Cross program. Perhaps this particular flowering has been cultivated by the most hands of all, and very devoted ones. It was after World War I, when women by the thousands had been doing Red Cross work, that the women of the boards of home and foreign societies developed a White Cross program for both overland and overseas missions.

White Cross is said to bless those who give, those who serve, and those who receive. Thousands of women have felt the joy of giving things made with their own hands to people thus made real to them. Missionaries' work has been supported by the contributions, and they have rejoiced to be able to share these gifts with people. Recipients of the bandages, handmade garments, baby things, and quilt blocks have felt befriended by the unknown women who stitched so firmly and rolled bandages so neatly.

Like all good programs long extended, White Cross frequently is called on to adapt. Some materials can now be bought more economically on the spot than sent from afar, and some fields no longer need supplies. But service of the same personal and individual sort, spread wider, is a never-ending imperative. The coordination of the White Cross kind of love with the United Nations kind of breadth could produce great gifts.

The report made in 1957 on the leadership role of ABHMS casts doubt upon the viability of the Christian Friendliness Department.

> Few of the executives [of states and cities] are aware of what the Christian Friendliness Program is about. Doubtless because of an earlier tradition of working through the women's organizations of the churches, this phase of the Society's program has not penetrated very far into the official structure of local agencies. . . .[3]

In an effort to make this phase of the Society's program penetrate further, the department was renamed in 1960 the Community Witness Program. This indicated a recognition of the need in our complicated society for a more politically astute approach. In 1966, to meet the acute need for minority representation, Atha Baugh was appointed the first man director, and the first department head. Dr. E. B. Hicks followed "Al" Baugh.

Matthew Giuffrida had been sharing in the work since 1955. Matt had returned from military service to enter peace service and had become the first male Christian Friendliness appointee. Under this department, Ruth Teasdale, Esther Davis, and he worked with the resettlement of refugees. This program, reflecting continual world chaos, has grown enormously. Since 1948, more than thirty thousand refugees have been placed, about half from Cuba, others from Eastern Europe, Indonesia, Burma, Hong Kong, Uganda, and Chile.

In 1965, Matt's work expanded. He is now administering the Parish Witness Program, which offers many services, including the Volunteer Services Program, which has placed several hundred young and older people in useful work all over the world for brief periods, sometimes extending into permanent assignments. The Parish Witness Program's success in placing Conscientious Objectors in alternative service assignments, the first time our denomination has performed such a ministry, has been so notable that the department is now empowered by the Selective Service System to make its own arrangements without prior approval. More than a hundred young students have benefited from international youth exchange projects sponsored by this program.

A recent significant appointment by the Parish Witness Program is that of Julia Ester Rivera-Ortiz as a program representative. She is the first woman of Latin American descent to be appointed to a national-level executive post in any ABC agency.

Women, as well as the men now largely in charge, can take pride in the continuing program of Parish Witness. Its objectives include the initial goals of Christian Americanization and Christian Friendliness, but they go beyond these. Partly, this is the increment of past accomplishments. Self-expression and revelation by the newly empowered minorities enrich and enlighten. For example, Australia Elcock, now administering in New York City Urban Friends Unlimited, a regional program and a successor to the old Camp Friendly Programs (in which largely minority-group children were invited to summer vacations with largely white rural hosts), brings to the task an understanding which the most discerning white leader would scarcely have.

The need to "facilitate the empowerment of minority and marginalized people and nationality groups to achieve self-development and cultural fulfillment" (one of the updated objectives stated by the Parish Witness Program and endorsed by the Division of Parish Development) had not earlier been fully comprehended. Nor was there so conscious an effort to realize what other cultures had to contribute. Meanwhile, the call to every individual is still central: "To offer service opportunities designed to make cultural institutions accountable to Christian standards of justice and ecological stewardship."[4]

We must no longer minister *only* person-to-person, but also *people-to-people*.

The late Roy Cunningham said that he felt that, though it was good when thousands of volunteers served hundreds of people, now we might all contribute, through our own intervention where possible, and through delegation of power, to the improvement of life for all God's children.

# 10
# The Pruning

"...a Paris idler who once took a walk in the Versailles Gardens concluded that, judging from all he saw, the trees grew ready trimmed."[1]

Stendhal

*Where have all the women gone?*

Since the integration of the WABHMS with the ABHMS, this question has been asked. First it was whispered, then murmured, and then shouted.

Merging the women's societies with the general societies had long been discussed and was firmly rejected by the women as early as 1902. But the question kept coming up, "Why should there be two Home [or Foreign] Mission Societies?"

The historical answer was, of course, that the appointment of single women missionaries to work among women and children had not even been attempted by the general boards, and the women had had to organize to fill this need. Later the women's societies had undertaken projects like Hospital Bautista in Managua, Nicaragua, and the Children's Homes in Kodiak, that included supervision of both men and women missionaries doing work for women and men. In a good many cases, the two boards had worked together on single projects, such as schools and Christian Centers. It became clear that there was duplication when such organizations had to be visited by two secretaries instead of one, and reports had to be written to two boards.

As Dorothy Bucklin says, "The WABHMS had an enormous portfolio—150 missionaries. We had the same work as the General Board, but smaller. We simply had to plan together for mature administration."[2] Even though, she adds, both men and women had their qualms.

Certainly the women hesitated. They handled things differently from the men, and they liked their own methods. They cherished their more intimate approach. While the General Society delegated much responsibility to state conventions and city societies in 1910, the women did not adopt this change until 1930.

Their supervisors "lived in" on field trips, stopping for several days at lonely outposts, absorbing the details of the needs and possibilities instead of just the broad outlines. On the other hand, perhaps for this reason they did not see the broad outlines quite so well as the men department heads, who covered the field more sweepingly, stopping at a central point, and summoning the field workers to come to them. If the women were sometimes hampered by the painstaking interest not only of their staff but also of their board members, the men often felt deprived because of the impersonality of their supervision.

The women had strengths, and they knew it. To them it seemed more important that the children enjoy themselves than that the Christian Center furniture be preserved. And they remembered that Mrs. Peabody, assistant secretary of WABFMS, had said that women should be left to their own methods and their own societies

> . . . unless the church has large tasks to assign to its women with the same freedom and representation given to men. No great plan of men which weakens or lessens this work of women or removes from them responsibility and initiative really marks a gain.[3]

However, the WABHMS finally agreed to a preliminary stage of unification. Their executive, Margaret Wenger, and G. Pitt Beers, executive of the ABHMS, agreed to locate analogous departments of the two societies side by side instead of keeping each organization in a bloc. When an official of one society resigned or retired, the remaining one was to take over both posts. It did happen that it was always the male secretary who remained. This was not accepted with equanimity by the missionaries in the field.

"There was something which I called 'a woman's voice' which was soon missing," says Margaret Wenger. "I lobbied for it in all the deliberations of the Committee on Integration. I had not forgotten that when I went to Mexico and Central America in 1948, I was an event, for both the nationals and the missionaries. They had not been visited by a woman for so long, and they depended on her insight and understanding to report their situation to members of the Board."

In 1953, in moods ranging from delight to despair, the women agreed to active negotiations, and by 1955 the integration was completed by a vote of the two societies at the Convention in Atlantic City. Each retained its legal identity, with its own constitution.

But for some reason, the contemplated provision for alternating men and women in the highest posts, which had been done in the Home Missions Council, was not made official. Of the current executives of the two societies at that time, the man was given the top job and the woman was given a newly created, subordinate, post. There has never since been a female executive secretary for any of the denominational agencies.

Helen Schmitz Collins, regional WABHMS supervisor, says:

> Did integration strengthen the woman's influence? Well, no! But there was some holding power, as on the Board of Managers, and there women supported notable improvements. Before integration, women were still receiving $4000 a year while men got $14,000. In 1956, equal pay was voted in and appeared in the minutes. Annual raises were to be given until the person reached the maximum pay for a particular position. However, the women secretaries had started out at such a low level they had to work a long time before reaching the maximum. On the other hand, new employees came in at the going rate. The imbalance will take time to equalize. The good intention of equal pay for equal work does not come through in reality—in the church or out.[4]

But Mrs. Collins feels that financial affairs were established on a much better basis and have been carried on efficiently. For example, the American Baptist Extension Corporation (ABEC), which does so much good in enabling building of various kinds, has been businesslike but helpful—"lovingly hard-boiled."

The influence of women, gravely undermined by the integration, lessened through the next years. As the apprehensive had foreseen, there was failure in the recuitment of women as missionaries and staff, in provision for experience to lead up to responsible positions, and in opportunity for advancement. On the managerial level, the number of women dropped from fifteen in 1958 to seven in 1970, and the number of women department heads dropped from ten to two.

Lack of professional opportunities in program and management inhibited the movement of women from the ranks to the staff which had been so notable in the past. Violet Rudd started her career in her local church in Bellingham, Washington. From there she went into association work. Berkeley Baptist Divinity School was her next step; after graduation she was a competent contender and natural choice for staff employment and professional advancement. But between 1963 and 1969, opportunities for women on staffs of regional and state conventions and city societies decreased at least 50 percent. These and other data were compiled by Elizabeth Miller, Secretary of the Division of Social Ministries, in a brochure called *Retreat to Tokenism.*

Where have *all* the women gone?

This is not just a Baptist question; the question serves as the title of a pamphlet by Marian Derby of the United Methodist Board of Missions. The historical content of her paper is based on Dr. R. Pierce Beaver's book, *All Loves Excelling,* which tells about the rise and fall of Women's Foreign Missionary Societies—paralleling the story of the Home Mission Societies.

Marian Derby's paper sets forth the decline of women's influence in the Protestant world mission in the last forty years. This includes the decrease in numbers of single women on the missionary staff and as mission executives and correlates this decrease with the ebb of missionary zeal in the churches.

In 1925, there were 4,824 North American single women missionaries out of a total of 13,555. In 1966, there were 4,828 out of more than 28,000, proportionately half as many.[5]

Dr. Beaver feels that the most potent factor in these losses has been the termination of a distinctive women's missionary movement carried out through women's agencies. Another loss directly attributable to this termination has been the decline of services to women and girls all over the world. And in addition, Dr. Beaver thinks, a quality of adventure and innovativeness has been lost to the mission movement, for he believes that women were often highly experimental in policy and strategy, and readier than men to take risks.[6]

*Where* have all the women gone? Surely they have not simply scampered away, allowing themselves to be eliminated without a struggle! There must have been skirmishes, holding actions.

Though the discouraging conclusions drawn above were made by United Methodists, that is the denomination in which the women have been more tenacious than in most. Their Women's Division still retains control of its program and policies and its right to raise and expend money. But major reorganization in 1964 eroded the initiative of women, when it combined the administration of women's work and general mission work.

Society at large, not just churches, has suffered the same regression in acceptance and use of women's talents. The earning gap between men and women in the fifteen years between 1955 and 1970 has widened. Women's median earnings in 1955 were 63.9 percent of men's; by 1970 they were only 59.4 percent. In every occupation, men, in 1968, were earning more than women doing the same work. This was true despite the fact that the average woman worker is slightly better educated than the average man worker, having completed 12.5 years of school to the man's 12.4. In 1920, women earned 16 percent of all the doctorates, in 1960–1969, 11.6 percent.

Then *why* have all the women gone?

The sustained seventy-year effort of the suffragettes triumphed in the Woman's Suffrage Act of 1920 and the Volstead Act. Now women had the power to change the country. And indeed, some laws for the protection of women and children did pass after women's suffrage, but not many. The watching politicians breathed a sigh of relief: the women were still women, reined in by fear of their husbands' and the world's opinions. Only a few years after their great achievement, women's influence in the secular world was at its lowest level. The Depression undercut any effort women might have made to progress in the working world; working women joined middle-class women in retreat.

Besides, a new era had dawned, which was stalemating men as well as women, an era of technical rationalization, of massive power, and intimidating bureaucracy. Since public life was becoming un-manageable, the individual began to take refuge in privatization, and women began to think about personal, inner freedom, and the psychiatric theories. Self-realization diverted their attention from the public duties they had felt responsible to before.

World War II seemed to change the situation entirely. Women were suddenly needed in the depleted labor force; it was revealed that they could even wield acetylene torches without destroying their femininity or the republic's manhood. Six million women were employed, even married women, and even women over thirty-five. Taboos vanished, it was thought forever. Hadn't it been laid down by Simone de Beauvoir that it would be through gainful employment, through ceasing to be a parasite, that woman would finally traverse the distance that separated her from the male?

But when the crisis passed, it was discovered that the taboos had not vanished at all. Women were still working, but they were working on the same low level as before. They had not been given better jobs. They had been hampered in the jobs they did have, because the United States government had not, like the British government, provided for child-care, which meant that women workers had a double burden almost unknown to men. Labor unions laughed at their efforts to gain membership; so they had no champions in cases of injustice. Besides, women were still afflicted with lack of confidence in this new realm of work, where men had reigned so long.

Women did not stop working. In 1970, there were thirty-two million women in the labor force. Women have had an increasing need to earn as inflation increases and standards of living soar. Two salaries are deemed necessary in many families, and the one-parent family is on the increase. But women have been undeniably pressed backward on the advance sectors during the past thirty years. It was probably easier for Elizabeth Blackwell to get into Geneva College Medical School in the 1840s than for a young woman in the 1960s. Since real vocational advance was so difficult, many women viewed a job as a rather unfortunate necessity, from which the fortunate escaped into domesticity.

The church reflects the world. The women's boards probably were anachronisms, excrescences on the streamlined ideal organization of the future. But women were no anachronisms. They never had been. And despite their sudden disappearance from prominence, they have not really vanished, nor been irrevocably dispersed.

Women are in the churches in larger proportion than men, just as they always have been. And they have carried on the spirit and cohesiveness of the auxiliaries that predated the mission societies and produced and sustained them. The societies recognized their value: "A vice-president in every state, a director in every association, a branch in every church, and every woman a contributor" was the goal of the Chicago Society.

In 1909, the Chicago and Boston Societies merged into WABHMS, and together with the WABFMS, in 1921, organized the Committee of Conference, with representatives from both boards. This gave them a more unified approach to the local woman's societies.

In 1937, there was a further reorganization, resulting in the National Committee on Woman's Work (NCWW), which gradually enlarged its scope to cover all phases of united missionary effort among Baptist women. Every two years the Foreign and Home Societies alternated responsibility for the office of chairman, secretarial work, and program. Each year this organization prepared, printed, and distributed program materials for the local societies, in cooperation with the Department of Missionary Education of the

Board of Education and Publication, which followed the annual mission study themes agreed upon by the interdenominational missionary education movement.

A good working relationship with state and city presidents was institutionalized by associate board memberships, and in 1945 the NCWW accorded membership to state presidents.

The National Council of American Baptist Women, formed in 1951 under the leadership of lay women within the denomination, with Violet Rudd serving as the executive director, has carried on the sustaining work of the past and developed a broad program dealing with family and community problems and needs that are at the heart of the mission.

Because of this stable and well-functioning organization, many church women were not immediately disturbed by the results of the reorganization. Their own roles had not been discredited, and if their organizations seemed to grow smaller and found it harder to attract response and get officers, they blamed it on society: "so many women work"; "the younger women aren't interested"; or "there are so many other organizations." But the worried few carried complaints to places of power. They put down the facts. They soon won a response from the Board of National Ministries.

If in 1958 there were fifteen women on the managerial level and in 1970 only seven, by 1974 the trend had reversed and there were nineteen. Thirty percent of the staff of the Board of National Ministries (the continuation of WABHMS-ABHMS) were women by 1974. An Affirmative Action Plan adopted a clear-cut salary policy, placing jobs on a grid structure without reference to sex. Implementation of an equal pay scale was undertaken several years before it became what it now appears to be, a popular necessity.

Paul Madsen, associate executive secretary of the Board of National Ministries, has as one of his responsibilities chairmanship of the Commission on the Ministry; in this capacity he has been carrying to local churches the need for placing women in pulpits, electing them as moderators, and placing them in other positions of influence in the church. He has received encouraging reactions from men as well as women and also some determined rejections, by women as well as men. The struggle seems to be gaining ground, but it has not yet prevailed.

Pruning can be wholesome to stimulate growth. Probably the separate agencies for women which were so effective in their time would now produce extra verbiage, depleting strength. But it's tragic to assume, as the Paris idler did in the Gardens of Versailles, that trees come ready trimmed—that women are prefabricated for certain limited roles.

And when growth of any part is cut back too drastically, the whole organism can be destroyed.

# 11

# The Fruit

We dedicate ourselves,

To the dream of the glorious Golden City, where all may live their lives in comfort, unafraid; a city of justice where none shall prey on others; a city of plenty where vice and poverty shall cease to fester; a city of brotherhood where all success shall be founded on service; a city of peace where order shall not rest on force, but on the love of all for the city, the great mother of the common life and weal. . . .[1]

The World Conference of Women in 1895 began with a solemn service, with a processional, hymn-singing, plainsong, a religious meditation by a delegate from the National Council of Jewish Women, and a litany of which the opening quotation was a part.

The liturgy expressed the confidence of women in what had been called both the "Protestant Century" and the "Woman's Century."

Page Smith, in his book *Daughters of the Promised Land,* writes: "One of the most important outlets for the Protestant passion in nineteenth-century America was the foreign and domestic mission field. . . . Like every reform movement of the age, women were in the forefront."[2]

Their U.S. schools for freed people were unique. Their mission schools abroad trained 70 percent to 90 percent of the elites who, after independence, came to dominate the course of the developing world. Their fight against injustice to minorities, while never decisive, has always been ameliorative.

In 1910, ten thousand women, half of them unmarried, worked in seventeen mission fields. Of them, 332 were physicians, "fired with a holy passion" for the rescue and empowerment of women in every society.

That is the past. But that flourishing tree, with its deep roots, wide branches, and beautiful flowering, has lately been drastically pruned by technology, by nationalism, and by declining religious and missionary zeal. Women have suffered a rout from responsibility. Is there hope for rebirth?

When women began to notice that they were being done out of their privilege of responsibility, they were appalled. One of the first areas of awareness, as Elizabeth Miller points out, was the vocational frustration of women seminary students. At the 1966 and 1967 Seminary Seniors' Conference, it was baldly revealed that nobody seemed to care whether the women graduates got jobs or not.

Graduates of BMTS with the Bachelor of Religious Education degree had been welcomed in the churches as directors of religious education since time immemorial; now it was brought out that since the fifties, this opportunity had eroded almost completely. Job descriptions had changed; assistant ministers were in demand, which implied a man who could preach part-time and invest the church with more prestige.

The women who wanted pastoral jobs got the smallest and last and worst. Ordination itself was an ordeal, even though Baptist attitudes are more enlightened than those of most denominations. Baptists have been ordaining women for more than eighty years, Presbyterians only since 1930, and Episcopalians still only with turmoil and schism. But there have never been more than twenty-five or thirty women in Baptist pastorates at any one time, a number which has never showed a consistent upturn.

Women were used to the ban on the pulpit, having always cheerfully passed the closed gates and taken up their work in the open fields. Why, now, did the flare of anger pass from one to another until it blazed up across the whole horizon? Their time had come!

In January, 1968, the Board of Managers of the American Baptist Women engaged in a seminar on Women in Church-Related Vocations. They sent out questionnaires to other women to consolidate their facts and inform their constituency.

In January, 1969, the Division of Christian Social Concern with the ABW (others on the national staff cooperating) initiated a study. Findings resulted in the formation of the American Baptist Executive Staff Women's Organization.

In 1970, this group presented recommendations to all agencies in the Convention, and in 1971, the Executive Committee of the Board of Managers made this recommendation:

That the Board and staff of the Societies seek to fill staff positions so that women will be appointed/employed to fill at least twenty-five percent of all positions at all staff levels below that of Executive Secretary: and that in the appointment/employment of staff women, salaries and annual increments equate with those of men staff with comparable preparation in comparable positions.

The women had been angry and got some action. But anger, though useful for what it can reveal, must be followed by clarification and redemption. The women turned to the question of *why*. They took a new kind of look at their religion, a theological look, and found that the Scriptures themselves explained why the ordination of women was so grudging, why the ministry of women was so confined, why the trust in women was so weak. Just as the Civil Rights movement suddenly discovered the hidden significance of imagery (black/white, light/darkness) and its effect in prolonging attitudes, so the women discovered that in the Bible *he* is the pronoun of honor and *man* comprehends all humanity. Is this the message of God to his children?

At the Grailville conference, Loveland, Ohio, in June, 1972, a group of women were assembled by Church Women United to "explore theology." The guests had been invited on the basis of their substance, knowledge, and accomplishments. Yet they began as little children, unstructured, receptive to each other, open to all possibilities. "We expected revelation, and we experienced it," says Emma Trout, a recent graduate of Colgate Rochester/Crozer/Bexley Hall. They wrote:

> In women's liberation Pentecost is ours also because it concerns the empowering of the formerly scattered, isolated, obscure, and unheard. It is as women have come and spent time together that they have found released among them, like a great rush of wind from heaven and like the flames of fire distributed to all, the utterance of a new language and strange speech, as each has found courage to express her thoughts in her own authentic words. Across the barriers of age, social class, culture and race, they speak and are heard. The customary hierarchies collapse as the voiceless find voice and the powerless power.[3]

This was not written by one person. It was a group expression. Women's theology here was not only a group contribution, but a group experience.

While this self-conscious *woman's* scrutiny of the Bible was attended by a sense of shock at the assumption of male superiority they found, deeper study brought new meanings. Phyllis Trible, the only woman full professor of a Baptist seminary at the time, has done scholarly studies of various passages. Hers is one of the first female interpretations, which shows new depths and evocative implications.

In his fascinating study, *Jesus Was a Feminist,* Leonard Swidler, of Temple University's Department of Religion, reminds us that in Jesus' time the status of women in Palestine was low. The "Queen of the Sabbath" was not allowed to join in the prayers. In fact, one daily prayer still in use today was a threefold thanksgiving that God "has not created me a gentile . . . a woman . . . an ignorant man." Women not only were restricted in prayer but also they received no social equality or independence.[4]

Yet Jesus, throughout the Gospels, spoke often of women, was concerned about them, and chose some of them as friends and confidantes. It was to a woman that he first appeared after his resurrection, and he commissioned her to tell the eleven. He healed a woman, Jairus's daughter, and two men who were dear to women he knew, the widow's son at Nain and Mary and Martha's brother Lazarus. He twice rejected the idea that women are merely sex objects instead of persons—when the woman of ill repute washed his feet, and when the scribes and Pharisees proposed to stone the woman taken in adultery. He taught the Samaritan woman, though even speaking to a woman was a breach of conduct, and it was to her that he first revealed himself as Messiah.

Jesus regarded marriage as an equally serious obligation to both men and women. And he regarded thinking in women to be respected, as demonstrated in the story of Mary and Martha. Further, when the woman in the crowd implied that his mother was blessed because she had borne him, he refused to equate the highest purpose of woman with motherhood. "Blessed rather are those who hear the word of God and keep it!" (Luke 11:28)[5]

Proof-text methods of sustaining a thesis are treacherous, because the Bible's breadth offers such unlimited possibilities for individual interpretation. But Jesus' firm assumption that women were intrinsically valuable and worthy of respect, as well as the whole spirit of his ministry, gives women's claims unimpeachable authority.

The women's new interest in theology has stirred them to action. "Our reason for being here is to find the way to say 'God loves you' to every person on earth. . . . The special task of church women is: *to serve as advocates for the powerless and helpless."*[6]

In the Articles of Incorporation of the Woman's American Baptist Home Mission Society, as amended in 1970, we find this statement:

The object of this Society shall be to proclaim and witness to the Christian

Faith in the United States and elsewhere in North America through the establishment, maintenance and assistance of churches, missions, and institutions of care or learning; to promote spiritual life and worship; and *to minister to persons of special need* in all ways its Board of Managers may deem appropriate.[7]

The phrase italicized by the author appears only in the *woman's* statement. It is their distinctive emphasis. And they have begun to emphasize it again as if it were a new thing, as indeed it always is.

The call to women is unlimited. It is a call to take an equal share in shaping the new society— the Golden City. "For as many of you as were baptized into Christ have put on Christ. There is neither Jew nor Greek, there is neither slave nor free, there is neither male nor female; for all are one in Christ Jesus" (Galatians 3:27-28).

Throughout the women's new activity there throbs an excitement and energy that reminds us of the Civil Rights movement, that reminds us of the Woman's Century and the audacity of Joanna P. Moore and Isabel Crawford and all those hundreds of other women who carried the good news.

Typical of the new initiatives expressed by women is the family education plan developed by Dr. Margaret Sawin of Rochester, New York. This is carried on by means of shared experiences through Family Clusters, which mutually support and teach each other over an extended period. They are led by trained experts in interpersonal relations.

An example of the determination of women to retrieve functional effectiveness is their determination to have more voice in how the money is spent; the ABW suggest that they control an amount equal to 10 percent of what they raise every year in Love Gift offerings.

Women's new initiative has been recognized in other areas than proposals for fair hiring and equal pay. In March, 1974, the women were *invited* to conduct a Leadership Development Program for the American Baptist Men.

The women themselves have been responsive. Professional women who once were bored by the Woman's Society activities are suddenly taking another look. "I haven't related to the Woman's Society, but now I see that I need them and they need me," they say. Women who tended to scorn those of their number who settled for, or rejoiced in, traditional domestic roles are now respectful of those preferences as long as they really are the woman's own choice.

"I think women should be allowed—without any restrictions—to work in any area they want," said Sara Darter, a student at Union Seminary who intends to be a parish minister.

She continued:

> We do have to be aware of the fact that historically women have by and large been limited to women's work and child-oriented and service professions. Women at this point in history that do choose the nurturing and homemaking professions may be expressing a defensiveness. All women should examine the factors and motives that lead them to where they are. We need to ask ourselves, am I being the most responsible steward I can?[8]

Sara was a lively participant in the Malvern Conference of Church Related Women in January, 1974. This conference resulted from several years of planning, initially backed by the M & M Board, which has under its charter of "Better Maintenance for the Ministry" a built-in concern for ordained women and missionaries, which it was very early in recognizing. A dozen women, after many consultations with executives at Valley Forge, formed a Steering Committee of American Baptist Professionally Employed Women. One of their first projects was to bring together at Malvern about seventy women from all over the country: older missionaries, young seminarians, moderates, and militants. They achieved a marvelous consensus after frankly and warmly differing on many points.

For example, a missionary from the Philippines revealed that women on that field suffer little limitation, while young women pastors across this country find fellow ministers treating their most serious contributions with levity.

A new opportunity for women pastors is the chaplaincy. A few women have been serving in recent years in hospitals and correctional facilities as chaplains. In 1972 the military chaplaincy opened up for women, and the Presbyterians were first to place a woman in this field of ministry. In 1973 Lorraine Potter became the first American Baptist woman endorsed for the military chaplaincy and is the first female chaplain in the Air Force. In 1974 Linda Jordan became the second American Baptist woman endorsed for the military chaplaincy and is now the second female chaplain in the Air Force. These pioneers will be followed by other American Baptist women still in training.

Professional women of wide experience, like Violet Rudd or Miriam Corbett (now director of Retirement Services for the M & M Board, formerly associate to Don Cloward in the Council for

Christian Social Progress), are refreshed and stimulated by the determined advance of young women on all fronts; they give full support as the girls battle real discrimination on many sides.

"The young women are hurting," Miriam says. They are still finding barriers across the way and wincing from slings and arrows. Admonitions to "Stay with the denomination!" and "Hang in there!" from these experienced and successful women really help when the scholarships are withdrawn, jobs are withheld, or projects are rejected.

So Emma Trout is persevering, working on her doctorate in Pastoral Counseling at Princeton. She says it may be that former frustrations have deepened her understanding and prepared her for better service. She wants to contribute to women's gain in initiative and power, but not in separation from men.

Sara Darter is determined to go ahead and act on her convictions without self-deprecation or trying to fit a male model; she believes she's perfectly OK as a woman.

Women seem about to reimmigrate into the larger world. They will then be obliged to go forward side by side with men on a harder journey than ever before. The intractability of history has revealed itself; and we see that it will yield only to the sustained and painful efforts of all of us working together. But the glory of history has also dawned upon us as we look back. None of our human failures can conceal the fact that our faith is an unlosable treasure. The tree is still alive, after severe pruning, and just ready to bear new fruit.

However, women need to be aware that as they attain power they must guard against becoming oppressive to anyone else. They should analyze the missionary achievements of their forerunners with respect, but also with relentless clarity. The same women who devoted themselves completely to the saving of souls and performance of acts of charity often overlooked the possibility of revelation from those whom they taught or the possibility of working to change the oppressive corporate and government policies that were short-circuiting their efforts.

We all, men and women alike, must realize that, though we plant and cultivate, the fruit is of God. In our efforts together, however good and strong, there is no place for men's pride; there is no place for women's pride; there is no place for human pride.

# Notes

**Chapter 1**

[1] Henrietta Buckmaster, *Let My People Go* (Boston: Beacon Press, 1959), p. 305.

[2] Joanna P. Moore, *In Christ's Stead* (Chicago: Women's Baptist Home Mission Society, 1903), p. 23.

[3] *Ibid.,* italics added.

[4] *Ibid.,* p. 24.

[5] Quoted by Noble Young Beall, "Northern Baptists in Higher Education for Negroes during 1865–1875." Original typewritten manuscript is located in the American Baptist Historical Society.

[6] W. E. B. Du Bois, *The Souls of Black People,* quoted by James M. McPherson, "White Liberals and Black Power in Negro Education 1865–1915." Unpublished manuscript available in Colgate Rochester Divinity School library.

[7] Moore, *op. cit.,* p. 26.

[8] *Ibid.,* p. 31.

[9] *Ibid.,* pp. 48, 61.

[10] *Ibid.,* p. 74.

[11] *Ibid.,* p. 88.

[12] *Ibid.,* p. 104.

[13] *Ibid.,* p. 106.

[14] *Ibid.,* p. 131.

[15] *Ibid.,* p. 152.

[16] *Ibid.,* pp. 159, 161.

[17] From a letter to the author from Mrs. Robert Caver.

[18] Moore, *op. cit.,* p. 126.

[19] *Ibid.,* p. 240.

[20] "Poverty-Stricken Childhood Influenced Attorney," *The State,* Columbia, South Carolina, March 20, 1973.

**Chapter 2**

[1] Charles L. White, *A Century of Faith* (Valley Forge: Judson Press, 1932), p. 22.

[2] Isabel Crawford, *Joyful Journey* (Valley Forge: Judson Press, 1951), p. 117.

[3] *Ibid.,* pp. 66-67.

[4] *Ibid.,* p. 67.

[5] *Ibid.,* pp. 77-78.

[6] *Ibid.,* p. 79.

[7] Quoted from Isabel Crawford's unpublished notebooks.

[8] *Ibid.*

[9] *Ibid.*

[10] "Termination" is a term which refers to the period when the Bureau of Indian Affairs was trying to terminate the responsibility of the federal government for the health and welfare of the Indians. It was energetically opposed by most church groups.

[11] Stan Steiner, *The New Indians* (New York: Dell Publishing Co., Inc., 1968), p. 6.

[12] Crawford, *Joyful Journey,* pp. 131-132.

[13] Vine Deloria, Jr., *We Talk, You Listen* (New York: The Macmillan Company, 1970), p. 83.

### Chapter 3

[1] Quoted from letters which are located in the Woman's American Baptist Home Missions' files.

[2] *Ibid.*

[3] *Ibid.*

### Chapter 4

[1] Mary Burdette, ed., *Home Missions Lessons,* a brochure which was produced by the Woman's Baptist Home Mission Society.

[2] *Ibid.*

[3] *Ibid.*

[4] *Ibid.*

[5] *Ibid.*

[6] The following quotations are taken from an interview by the author with Luella Adams Killiam Funk.

### Chapter 5

[1] *Home Mission Monthly,* September, 1892, p. 307.

[2] Quoted from the records of the Board of the Baptist State Convention of California, 1880.

[3] *Ibid.*

[4] Quoted from a letter to the author from Dr. James Chuck.

[5] Quoted from an interview by the author with Astrid Peterson.

[6] Quoted from an interview by the author with Amy Purcell.

[7] *Ibid.*

[8] Quoted from an interview by the author with Bernice Cofer.

[9] Bill Hosokawa, *Nisei: The Quiet Americans* (New York: William Morrow & Co., Inc., 1969), p. 337.

[10] Quoted from an interview by the author with Bernice Cofer.

### Chapter 6

[1] Quoted from *Home Missions Lessons,* a brochure which was produced by the Woman's Baptist Home Mission Society.

[2] Marian Parker, "Colegio Bautista in Managua, Nicaragua," *Missions,* vol. 21, no. 5 (May, 1930), p. 291.

[3] Quoted from a letter written by Mary Butler.

[4] Grace Hatler, *Land of the Lighthouse* (Valley Forge: Judson Press, 1966), pp. 55-63.

[5] Quoted in a letter received from Roberto Porras, a Mexican pastor.

[6] Quoted from a speech delivered by Edward Kennedy in April, 1970, in an article by William Wipfler, "Latin America: U.S. Colony," *Christianity and Crisis,* April 3, 1972, p. 68.

[7] Rafael Cepeda, "The Cuban Lesson," reprinted from *TEMPO,* a publication of the National Council of Churches. Used with permission.

[8] LÁ DOC: II, 19a, taken from *Diálogo Social.*

### Chapter 7

[1] Joanna P. Moore, *In Christ's Stead* (Chicago: Women's Baptist Home Mission Society, 1902), p. 140.

[2] Quoted from the minutes of the meeting of the Women's Baptist Mission Society of Michigan, 1873.

³Quoted from the "Report of Executive Board of the Women's Home Mission Society" of Chicago, 1878, p. 27.

⁴Quoted from the minutes of the meeting of the Woman's American Baptist Home Mission Society, Boston, 1877, p. 1.

⁵Quoted from the "Report of Executive Board of the Women's Baptist Home Mission Society," 1878, p. 27.

⁶Quoted by Bertha Grimmel Judd, *Fifty Golden Years*, p. 125.

⁷*Ibid.*, p. 126.

⁸"Voices from the Field," *Tidings*, August, 1883, pp. 1-2.

⁹*Ibid.*

¹⁰Quoted from an interview with Miss Rena Button.

## Chapter 8

¹Quoted from a letter from a migrant worker to the author.

²Joint Statement, 1924, of the Home Missions Council and the Council of Women for Home Missions.

³Robert Handy, *We Witness Together* (New York: Friendship Press, 1957), p. 106.

## Chapter 9

¹Mary Martin Kinney, *The World at My Door* (Valley Forge: Judson Press, 1938), p. 20.

²Rachel DuBois and Mew-soong Li, *Know Your Neighbors* (New York: The Workshop for Cultural Democracy, 1955), Foreword.

³Quoted from the Report made in 1957 on the Leadership Role of the American Baptist Home Mission Society.

⁴Quoted from the Parish Witness Program Report, January 15, 1973, p. 2.

## Chapter 10

¹Quoted in Simone de Beauvoir, *The Second Sex* (New York: Alfred A. Knopf, Inc., 1953), p. 224.

²Quoted from an interview with Dorothy Bucklin.

³Louise Cattan, *Lamps Are for Lighting* (Grand Rapids, Mich.: Wm B. Eerdmans Publishing Company, 1972), p. 115.

⁴Quoted from an interview with Helen Schmitz Collins.

⁵R. Pierce Beaver, *All Loves Excelling* (Grand Rapids, Mich.: Wm. B. Eerdmans Publishing Co., 1968), p. 199.

⁶*Ibid.*, pp. 199-200.

## Chapter 11

¹Page Smith, *Daughters of the Promised Land: Women in American History* (Boston: Little, Brown and Company, 1970), pp. 175-176.

²*Ibid.*, p. 181.

³Quoted from Winsome Munro, "Pentecost as a Paradygm for Women's Liberation." *Women Exploring Theology*, 1972, materials from the conference at Grailville.

⁴Leonard Swidler, "Jesus Was a Feminist," *Catholic World* (January, 1971), pp. 177-183.

⁵*Ibid.*

⁶Quoted from a brochure entitled *Calls to Citizen Action* (1971), published by Church Women United, pp. 2-3.

⁷Acts and Articles of Incorporation and By-Laws of The American Baptist Home Mission Society; Woman's American Baptist Home Mission Society, 1973.

⁸Quoted from an interview with Sara Darter.